DISCARDED

American Legal Institutions
Recent Scholarship

Edited by Eric Rise

A Series from LFB Scholarly

This Land is Your Land, This Land is My Land
The Property Rights Movement and Regulatory Takings

Alfred M. Olivetti, Jr., and Jeff Worsham

LFB Scholarly Publishing LLC
New York 2003

Copyright © 2003 by LFB Scholarly Publishing LLC

All rights reserved.

Library of Congress Cataloging-in-Publication Data

Olivetti, Alfred M.
 This land is your land, this land is my land : the property rights movement and regulatory takings / Alfred M. Olivetti, Jr., and Jeff Worsham.
   p. cm. -- (American legal institutions)
 Includes bibliographical references and index.
 ISBN 1-931202-41-9 (alk. paper)
  1. Eminent domain--United States. 2. Right of property--United States. 3. Environmental law--United States. I. Worsham, Jeffrey. II. Title. III. Series.
  KF5599 .O43 2002
  343.73'0252--dc21

2002152154

ISBN 1-931202-41-9

Printed on acid-free 250-year-life paper.

Manufactured in the United States of America.

To Keri
A.O.

To
Aka, Cupie, Imoto, Kuzo, and Hatu
J.W.

CONTENTS

	List of Illustrations	ix
	Acknowledgements	xi
1	Introduction	1
2	Changing the Tide of Events	5
3	Modern Environmentalism and the Property Rights Movement	21
4	The Courts as a Venue	49
5	The Property Issue in Congress	73
6	If at First you do not Succeed	117
	Appendix: Takings Legislation	133
	Notes	145
	References	149
	Index	165

ILLUSTRATIONS

FIGURES

5.1	The Legislative Agenda	77
5.2	House Public Lands Bill Referrals	79
5.3	Senate Public Lands Bill Referrals	80
5.4	House Wildlife Bill Referrals	82
5.5	Senate Wildlife Bill Referrals	83
5.6	House Public Lands Hearings	89
5.7	Senate Public Lands Hearings	91
5.8	Public Lands Hearing Competition	92
5.9	House Property Rights Hearings	94
5.10	Senate Property Rights Hearings	95

TABLES

5.1	The Correspondence Between Committee Venue and Type of Witness	98
6.1	Venue Shifting	123

ACKNOWLEDGEMENTS

Thanks to mom and dad for your unconditional love, encouragement, and support - not only during my Ph.D. years, but throughout my life. Your importance in my life is immeasurable and you both deserve credit for all that I accomplish. Thanks to Mike, Lisa, Vince, Stacey and our growing family for being great brothers, sisters, and friends. I am fortunate and proud to be surrounded by such a wonderful group of people. Thanks to Jeff Worsham whose support, guidance, and exceptional ability to conceptualize a study made all the difference in the world. Thanks also to John Kilwein, Chris Mooney, Chris Plein, and Neil Berch for their contributions in completing this study. Thanks to everyone within the department of political science at West Virginia University, especially Dr. Hammock and Lee Ann Greathouse, who made the tasks of being a graduate student more bearable and made it easy to walk the halls of the third floor with a smile. Thanks to my friends in Morgantown for allowing me to be part of a community that is never short of goodwill, humor, and miles of training. On On! Finally, thanks to all my close friends that have contributed to my life - I wish you all to know how lucky I feel that you are part of my life.

Al Olivetti

Thanks to graduate students (and colleagues) like Al, who make it all worth the effort. And as always, thanks to Deb.

Jeff Worsham

CHAPTER ONE

Introduction

The right to own property is a fundamental value in the United States, and the rights of the property owner are often considered paramount (Sax 1971; see Epstein 1985, for an extreme example of this argument). Still, the individual right to property is subject to limitations. Government can exercise its police power to control a public nuisance—actions that threaten the public safety and welfare or violate the rights of others—with no compensation due the offender. The power of eminent domain allows the government to seize the property of an individual to serve a vital public interest. In such cases, the right to redress is embedded in the last sentence of the Fifth Amendment, which holds that "no private property be taken for public use, without just compensation."

The Takings Clause, as this sentence is called, was extended to the states and their local subdivisions by the Fourteenth Amendment to the U.S. Constitution. The Due Process Clause of the Fourteenth Amendment states, "nor shall any State deprive any person of life, liberty, or property, without due process of law." From these two legal doctrines, individuals have begun to argue against regulation that results in less than an actual physical loss of property. Arguing that some governmental actions, ranging from land use planning restrictions to the enforcement of regulatory and species protection statutes, results in a "regulatory taking," they suggest that compensation is guaranteed for government actions that fall short of actual confiscation. Indeed, some property rights advocates go so far as to argue that a regulatory taking occurs whenever there has been a diminution in the market value of property caused by government action (Fellows 1996). This study is interested in exploring the origins and progress of this line of reasoning in the current debate centered on property rights.

We suggest that the regulatory takings issue provides an excellent case to study theoretical questions concerning agenda setting and the policy process, topics explored in the second chapter. In particular we are interested in the progress of property rights advocates in setting the agenda on matters pertaining to the regulation of public lands and species protection. We suggest that the property rights "movement" is part of a environmental backlash (Switzer 1997), that has gone through three distinct phases since the 1970s, a subject we explore in the third chapter. In that chapter we detail the rise of the modern environmental movement, discuss its institutionalization in the American polity, and show how a loose coalition of economic and ideological interests engage in a counter-mobilization in an effort to make an inroad into the "green" consensus. The efforts of the property rights movement to redefine the issue take place in

Introduction 3

three distinct venues—the courts, Congress, and the various state legislatures. Chapter four traces the legal history of the regulatory taking issue as addressed by the Supreme Court. The fifth chapter, which forms the heart of our analysis, tracks the property issue as it is addressed in Congress. We suggest that the economic use of public lands, and property rights, have never been out of fashion in Congress. We track the entrance of environmental and conservation concerns into the public lands subsystem, document the adjustments made to accommodate the institutionalization of these concerns, and conclude with an in-depth study of the attempts by property rights entrepreneurs to redefine the issue via legislation. In chapter six we conclude with a brief exploration of the property rights issue as it moves to the states.

CHAPTER TWO

Changing the Tide of Events

Ours is a study of setting the property rights agenda. As such, we begin by reviewing the literature on agenda setting, highlighting the interplay between public demands, government preferences, and the actual policies that result. An agenda is "the list of subjects or problems to which government officials, and people outside government closely associated with those officials, are paying serious attention at any given time" (Kingdon 1995, 3). Gaining agenda status is a primary objective of any group or interest supporting a specific issue, and rightfully so given the substantial stakes involved in gaining agenda status. Most importantly, those who build and control the political agenda play an instrumental role in structuring subsequent policy choices. This is no small matter given our pluralistic society in which interest groups compete for political influence (Truman 1951; Latham 1952; Becker 1983; Walker 1991).

The benefits of agenda control extend beyond policy influence. Agenda control also brings social recognition and the validation of certain values and beliefs to the exclusion of others (Cobb and Elder 1983; Jones 1993). When government decides to consider an issue it serves to validate the problem and lend credibility to the views held by those pressing the issue, as well as legitimizing its authority to address the issue. In light of government's capacity to consider only some issues, this consideration functions to determine the winners and losers in a social and political sense. Consequently, interests realize both personal satisfaction and public endorsement when their concerns are granted agenda status by government officials. In short, agenda control is an objective worthy of study given the political and social benefits that accrue to those who are successful at setting the agenda.

Agenda Types

Those who study agenda setting identify three agenda types. The first, the *systemic* or *public* agenda, "consists of all issues that are commonly perceived by members of the political community as meriting public attention and as involving matters within the legitimate jurisdiction of existing governmental authority" (Cobb and Elder 1983, 85). The systemic agenda is home to those concerns widely shared by members of the polity. As such, the content of the public agenda is shaped by the dominant norms and ideology of a community. Evidence that an item has made it to the systemic agenda include mention in public opinion polls and increased media attention. More often than not, an item on the public agenda does not come with a solution attached. Rather, the development of solutions awaits entrance on one of the other two agendas.

The second agenda type, the *institutional* or *government* agenda, consists of the list of items of concern to government officials (Kingdon 1995). While we often speak of the government agenda, it is more accurate to use the plural, and discuss government agendas. This is because in our system of separate institutions sharing power, there are arguably as many government agendas as there are government institutions. In the U.S. polity it is usually the case that an issue must first achieve public agenda status before ascending to the government agenda. This means convincing the public that your issue is, or should be, a national concern is fundamental to achieving agenda entrance. Even if an item reaches the systemic agenda there is no guarantee that policy makers will address the issue. A primary constraint on an issue's progression is the legitimacy of the group pushing the issue. Groups with low status, a lack of material resources, or who challenge dominant political norms, find it more difficult to gain entry to the government agenda (Cobb and Ross 1997).

Still, the government agenda can be accessed without an attempt to access the public agenda. Indeed, bureaucrats, select members of Congress, and private interests often move items directly to the government agenda because they do not need, or want, broader public support (Ripley 1985). When these subgovernments set the agenda, the last thing they desire is issue expansion, which risks arousing opposition (Cobb, Ross, and Ross 1976; Baumgartner and Jones 1993; Worsham 1997). An item may also reach the government agenda as a result of a crisis or disaster. The near meltdown at the Three Mile Island nuclear power plant in 1979 is a prime example. The accident, which threatened a release of radioactive fuel, provided a launching pad for the reconsideration of nuclear energy as a power source (Baumgartner and Jones 1993). Crisis situations immediately put something on the governmental agenda, regardless of public debate regarding the proper definition of the crisis.

Not all items on the governmental agenda receive serious attention from decision-makers. For instance, many bills introduced in the U.S. Congress have symbolic appeal for constituents, but are never considered in committees and consequently never reach the floor. Rather, it is when an item exists on multiple government agendas that agenda setting enters its final phase of attaching solutions to problems. This final phase involves yet a third agenda type, the *decision* agenda. The decision agenda consists of "that set of items explicitly up for active and serious consideration of authoritative decision-makers" (Cobb and Elder 1983, 86; Kingdon 1995). Items that reach this agenda are primed for government action. That is, at this point policy alternatives are usually available and the problems are directly identified. Consequently, decision agendas are more focused than the systemic or governmental agendas. The subject of discussion is which solution, or solutions, is/are an acceptable response to the problem at hand. For an item to be up for an 'active decision,' such as legislative enactment or presidential action, there must be a viable solution available for the decision makers to consider. Thus, only those problems that have a politically practical solution attached to them will be considered for government action. Paul Light's (1982) study of the president's agenda demonstrated that an item with an 'available alternative' invariably crowded out equally worthy subjects that did not have viable solutions.

As stated previously, there is no guarantee that an issue will reach agenda status at any of the three levels, or that achieving agenda status on one level guarantees a move to the next level. The fact remains that in the political game policy makers attend to some issues and not others, why this is so is the focus of those who study agenda setting, a subject to which we now turn.

Models of Agenda Setting

Agenda setting, or agenda building, refers to the process by which demands of various groups in the population are translated into items vying for the serious attention of public officials. Agendas are rarely stable. Rather, they fluctuate as problems are placed on the agenda, remain for some time, and then fade away as new problems appear and dominate attention. This ebb and flow of agenda status is referred to as agenda change. E.E. Schattschneider (1960) was among the first students of agenda setting to assert that the key to gaining the advantage in a social conflict was to affect both the type and number of groups participating in the process. Groups intent on changing the policy status-quo attempt to expand the scope of the conflict in order to disturb existing policy arrangements. This strategy is generally referred to as *issue expansion* and involves bringing in new interests that advocate for a re-division of the policy pie. The call for reallocating the benefits and costs of public policy is often accompanied by an effort at reinterpreting the origins of existing problems. In some cases previously agreed upon solutions are themselves subject to being defined as a problem. Since its initial enunciation, a variety of scholars have incorporated Schattschneider's observations into their models of agenda setting.

Cobb, Ross, and Ross (1976) discuss three processes of agenda building: *mobilization, outside initiative, and inside initiative*. The mobilization model describes a process whereby agenda building is initiated by political leaders who, after placing the item on the governmental agenda, try to promote the interest and support in the general public needed for the adoption of their issues. Thus, government officials attempt to expand the issue from the governmental agenda to the systemic agenda in the hopes of demonstrating its relevance to particular groups that may impede implementation and persuade them that the new program merits government action. The issue's expansion is the key strategy in the mobilization model.

The outside initiative model describes a process of agenda building whereby an interest group defines an issue as a problem and attempts to expand support for it's definition so that they can gain public, then systemic, and finally decision agenda status for their issue (Cobb, Ross, and Ross1976). As with the mobilization model, issue expansion is the key. The hope is that once the issue gains the support of additional groups, it will create enough pressure on authorities to force serious consideration of the issue on terms favorable to the initiating group.

The inside initiative model describes an agenda building process whereby issue expansion does not play a major role. In this scenario the most common origin of policy ideas are the multitude of subsystems that populate the policy landscape. Well- organized private interests work with the appropriate congressional committee and agency personnel to formulate policy in the mutual interest of all three players (Baumgartner and Jones 1993; Worsham 1997; Eisner, Worsham and Ringquist 2000). These policy monopolies do not seek public support for the innovation nor do they try to place the issue on the systemic agenda. Instead of formulating policy at the macro-level of the polity, which would involve creating public support for an issue, they work at the meso-level where congressional committees, career bureaucrats, and special interests reign supreme (Thurber 1991; McCool 1990).

John Kingdon's (1995) discussion of agenda setting focuses on the interaction among what he calls the *political, policy, and problem streams*. The streams metaphor is used to describe how solutions, problems, and opportunities to connect the two, often develop independently of one another. Solutions are developed in the policy stream by communities of issue specialists drawn from academia, interest groups, administrative agencies, and congressional committee staff. Kingdon draws on the garbage can model of Cohen, March and Olsen (1972) to suggest that solutions are continually developed, discussed, and rethought in the policy stream, whether or not they respond to an actual issue on one of the agendas. That is, solutions often predate the problems to which they are eventually attached. Kingdon labels these unattached solutions as the policy "primeval soup."

Developments in the political stream involve a variety of activities that may produce new perceptions of issues, redefining them as problems worthy of agenda entrance. Fluctuations in the 'national mood' or 'political climate,' a change in presidential administration, shifts in party control of either or both chambers of Congress, new personnel on the courts, or party realignment, may serve to promote new items on the governmental agenda and open the door for the consideration of solutions floating in the policy stream.

Finally, events in the problem stream may grab the attention of the public and policy makers. Change in select economic indicators, focusing events such as natural disasters or military hostilities, or feedback from implementation of current policy, can force government to consider an issue (Kingdon 1995). The problem stream recognizes that at times, "stuff happens," leaving government little choice but to respond.

At critical times the separate streams come together to impact the agenda and produce policy change. A problem is recognized, a solution is available, and the political climate is ripe for change. Kingdon (1995) refers to these moments of opportunity as *policy windows*. Policy windows are fleeting and often short lived occasions when events in the problem and/or political stream push some issues to the forefront of governmental attention. During these occasions *policy entrepreneurs* play an instrumental role in both agenda entrance and the attachment of a solution (or solutions) to the problem. Policy entrepreneurs develop strategies that allow them to shape the terms of discourse surrounding the problem and the proper solution to it (Riker 1986; Kelman 1987; King 1988; Smith 1991; Mintrom 1997). This often involves defining problems in such a way so as to assemble and maintain a majority coalition in support of a particular solution (Eyestone 1978; Smith 1991).

The Systemic Context of Agenda Setting

A focus on the details of agenda setting should not blind one to the importance of the larger setting in which events unfold. Andrew McFarland (1991) argues that the study of agenda setting can be viewed as a corollary to the study of political cycles. For example, David Truman's (1951) 'wave theory' argues that the mobilization of any interest provokes a counter mobilization of related or affected interests. In Truman's view, the American polity is characterized by regular waves of mobilization and counter mobilization, creating a cyclical pattern over time. Rather than explaining interest group mobilization as a response to other interest groups, Salisbury (1969) suggests such mobilization is reaction to 'disturbances' in the larger social and economic system itself. He argues that the

American political system goes through a cycle of rest, disturbance, and rest, in response to economic developments, technological changes, and similar system-level stimuli. Arthur Schlesinger's (1986) model of American political development has a similar systemic and cyclical focus. In Schlesinger's view, public policy oscillates between periods of rapid progressive governmental action and periods of conservative retrenchment. Similarly, Herbert McClosky and John Zaller (1984) identify thirty-year attitudinal swings between moods of 'capitalism' and 'democratic values.' In the former, entrepreneurs rely on anti-government, pro-market attitudes to set the policy agenda. In the latter, another set of entrepreneurs arouse democratic and public-minded attitudes in an effort to reorient the policy agenda. Finally, Andrew McFarland's (1991) cyclical model suggests that American politics is characterized by the creation of powerful subsystems backed by business interests. Over time these generate a policy reaction emphasizing consumer protection, democratic egalitarianism, and similar ideals. The result is a polity that cycles between special interests and public interest politics.

Baumgartner and Jones (1993) present the most fully developed systemic theory of agenda setting to date. Their 'dual mobilization' model suggests agenda access is achieved through 'waves of mobilization'. The first wave, or *Downsian mobilization*, is based upon Anthony Downs's 'issue attention cycle.' In Downs's (1972) approach, there is a pre-problem stage in which little attention is given to a problem, followed by a state of alarmed discovery and euphoria characterized by a good deal of public attention. This heightened attention produces a policy solution, which over time gives way to a realization of the costs of solving the problem and, finally, a gradual decline in public interest (Downs 1972).

Baumgartner and Jones (1993) emphasize the events occurring during the euphoria stage, when heightened public attention prompts government action to solve a problem. The resulting policy solution takes the form of new institutions developed to implement policy directives. Even after public attention that served to prompt government action fades away, the institutional arrangements remain (Peters and Hogwood 1985; Baumgartner and Jones 1993). These arrangements take the form of policy subsystems. Subsystems are a means of reaching policy agreement based on the mutual self-interest, shared policy perspective, or similar expertise of the participants. As such they seek to remove agenda setting activity from the macro-level of the polity, where the outside initiative model holds sway, and place it at the meso-level, where congressional committees (or subcommittees), administrative agencies, and well organized interests control the agenda.

The second wave of mobilization, which they describe as a *Schattschneider* mobilization, is a reaction to the policy produced as a result of a Downsian mobilization. During a Schattschneider mobilization opponents seek to redefine issues in terms that challenge the validity or appropriateness of existing policy. The goal of such activity is to dismantle or alter the subsystem arrangements created during the Downsian mobilization (Baumgartner and Jones 1993). Their model of *punctuated equilibrium* argues that subsystem arrangements, while producing long lasting policy equilibrium, are subject to rapid change when systemic events increase the salience of issues under their control.

Baumgartner and Jones (1993) "dual mobilization" theory suggests a cyclical pattern of political change in the United States much like that espoused in the cycle theories. However, they claim their depiction of a punctuated pattern, rather than a cyclical pattern, of policy change is more complete given the identification of an institutional legacy and its capacity to bring in fresh definitions of political issues. New issue definitions of familiar problems mean that the changes brought on by changes in the institutional structure are different from those that occurred before. Therefore, while the political mobilization of interests in American politics is a reaction to the existing political arrangements, it need not be related to the mobilizations of a generation before.

The review of the literature underscores the importance of issue expansion in agenda setting. In general, the previous models follow Schattschneider's lead in emphasizing the effects that an increase in participants and venues may have on agenda change. Cobb, et al's (1976) "mobilization" model and "outside initiative" model emphasize the utility of issue expansion in garnering support from new groups and moving the issue up on the systemic and governmental agenda. Kingdon's (1995) "problems" stream illustrates the important role played by policy entrepreneurs to expand an issue by framing it in such a manner to solicit as much support as possible. Our study of the regulatory takings issue follows Baumgartner and Jones's (1993) "dual mobilization" model that gives great weight to issue expansion, particularly during a

Schattschneider mobilization when it is used to fuel the effort to destroy the institutional structure that obstructs the policy goals of an interest. To be sure, issue expansion is critical in most cases of agenda setting.

Policy Images and Venues

The process of setting the agenda is not simply getting someone to pay attention to your issue. Rather, agenda setting involves manipulating how an issue is understood and discussed, or gaining acceptance of a particular *policy image* (Baumgartner and Jones 1993). Problems are socially constructed. As such their recognition and understanding arise from the meanings that people attach to the circumstances surrounding the problem. This means there are numerous possible interpretations of the same issue. The understanding that is eventually accepted as "real" is shaped not only by "facts," but also by select beliefs and values (Cobb and Elder 1983; Jones 1994). Beliefs and values determine what is to be taken as fact, which facts are considered relevant, and how those facts are interpreted (Sabatier and Jenkins-Smith 1993). Opposing interests attempt to frame the problem to further their objectives, while questioning the merit of competing definitions or understandings of the issue in question. This competition over opposing policy images is an ingrained part of politics and a defining component of the struggle for agenda control (Stone 1989; Baumgartner and Jones 1993; Jones 1994).

The struggle over a problem's *definition* has important consequences for its political standing and the eventual solutions attached to the problem (Rochefort and Cobb 1994; Kingdon 1995). Indeed, for Schattschneider (1960) a problem's definition was *the* critical factor in policymaking. Cobb and Elder (1983) suggest that participation in policy debate is increased when a problem is defined in ambiguous, non-technical, symbolic terms. Similarly, the definition of issues in procedural or narrowly technical terms restricts the scope of participation (Nelkin 1975). Problem definition occurs throughout the political system. That said, over time government institutions develop units that specialize in problem definition and the generation of solutions. These policy *venues* are "institutional locations where policy decisions are made" (Baumgartner and Jones 1993, 32).

Venue shifting is akin to agenda shopping in that policy advocates look around for a hospitable venue from which to launch their efforts. Venue shopping is important because "each institutional venue is home to a different image of the same question" (Baumgartner and Jones 1993, 31). Quite simply, congressional committees, the courts, bureaucratic agencies, the executive, state governments, and the like, all present venues which may subscribe to not only different policy images, but also favor particular groups (Baumgartner and Jones 1993; Worsham 1998). The choice of venue, then, often determines which groups will influence policy outcomes, the manner in which the issue is framed, and the nature of the public policy produced.

Policy specialization between the two levels of government (state/local and federal) also lends importance to venue shifting. As a fundamental feature of American Federalism, policy specialization allows the different levels of government to pursue different policy priorities. Research by Peterson (1981) and Peterson and Wong (1986) shows that state legislatures serve the economic interests that are dominant in the state more often than other state level institutions. In the intergovernmental context, state and local governments are pushed toward the pursuit of policies that promote economic growth, whereas the federal government is more likely to pursue policies that redistribute benefits toward disadvantaged citizens.

In sum, the venue in which an issue is considered matters greatly. Control over the proceedings of problem definition, especially with regard to who is involved, has a large impact on how the issue is framed and the solution(s) generated. Those interested in altering the content of public policy must not only find a seat at the table, they must do their best to influence what is on the menu as well.

Conclusion

The battle for agenda control of the property rights issue is being fought in multiple venues. While Congress serves as the major stage, state legislatures and the federal courts are also involved in the property rights drama. In the following chapters we employ the concepts of issue expansion, problem definition, and venue control to understand the struggle between the property rights community and their conservation and environmental opponents. In order to gain a stronger appreciation of the struggle for agenda control, the next chapter offers a brief history of the modern environmental movement. The chapter traces the development and institutionalization of environmental protection policy, suggesting that environmental concerns succeed in gaining permanent agenda status because they resonate on the public agenda. Equally important, they find an institutional niche in the congressional committee system. The success and institutionalization of the environmental movement in turn provokes a series of counter-mobilizations, each of which explores a different variation of property rights and none of which are successful in securing a spot on the decision agenda.

CHAPTER THREE

Modern Environmentalism and the Property Rights Movement

Robert Nisbet argues "[w]hen the history of the twentieth century is finally written, the single most important social movement of the period will be judged to be environmentalism"(Caldwell 1985, 259). While one might argue where environmentalism fits in the queue of social movements in the 20th century, there is little doubt it occupies an important place. Still, the legislative successes of the environmental movement have not been celebrated by everyone. As Schattschneider would predict, environmentalism has spawned a counter movement. Generally referred to as the *property rights movement,* this reaction is composed of a mixed group of grass-roots activists, political conservatives, and industry interests that seek to alter the regime of regulations governing conservation and environmental matters (Marzulla 1995).

In agenda setting language, the mobilization of the property rights community is a reaction to the policy consequences developing out of the environmental and conservation laws of the past three decades. Environmentalists justified government regulations with conservation, ecosystem and species protection, and quality of life arguments. The property rights community engaged in a Schattschneiderian mobilization by arguing against the economic burdens brought on by environmental regulations. In so doing, the property rights community framed the matter in economic and legal terms, and ultimately, as a question of individual liberty.

This chapter documents the action-reaction phenomenon associated with the evolution of the modern environmental and the property rights movements. It explains the role of environmental regulation in energizing the property rights movement by illustrating how the consequences of environmental achievements have fueled an antagonistic reaction from the property rights side.

Modern Environmentalism

Most observers credit the first Earth Day, April 22, 1970, as the beginning of modern environmentalism. In reality this landmark event was merely a response to a series of events throughout the 1960s that brought environmental issues to the attention of the public, and eventually policymakers. First, in 1962 Rachel Carson's *Silent Spring* focused public attention on the harmful impact of chemicals and pesticides, particularly DDT, on the environment. Carson's study of the use of chemicals and pesticides redefined the issue as a serious threat to the natural and human environment and marked the entry of modern environmentalism onto the public agenda. If before 1962 the use of pesticides was largely considered an agriculture and commercial issue, after the publication of *Silent Spring* it became a public concern. While a portion of the public was awakened by Carson and like-minded authors, two "eco-catastrophes" in 1969 heightened public awareness of threats to the environment. First, in January and February 1969, two oil spills off the coast of Santa Barbara, California demonstrated pollution was a regular, and disastrous, consequence of business as usual in much of American industry. The television and print media were filled with images of birds and pristine beaches destroyed by oil (Steinhart and Steinhart 1972). When Cleveland's Cuyahoga River burst into flames in the summer of 1969, the response was equally alarmed. Television sets across America exposed the incredible spectacle of the river burning from an abundance of toxic wastes and pollutants that saturated it, and more importantly were known to have existed for decades. While the images from Santa Barbara were shocking, some were willing to write them off as a once-in-a-lifetime cataclysmic event. When it came to the Cuyahoga, locals—and soon the nation—came to realize that pollution was the underside of industrial development. The Santa Barbara oil spills and the burning Cuyahoga river captured America's attention and marked the entry of environmental protection onto the systemic agenda.

These events, and others, reawakened a new environmental consciousness in America. The concern with the health and fate of the earth's natural resources was heightened by existing environmental groups, such as the Sierra Club, the National Audubon Society, the Wilderness Society, the National Parks and Conservation Association, and the National Wildlife Federation (NWF), which saw their membership rolls swell during the period. Moreover, between 1967 and 1971, many new environmental groups were formed such as the Environmental Defense Fund (EDF), Friends of the Earth, the Natural Resources Defense Council (NRDC), and Greenpeace USA. Working the grass roots, and lobbying in Washington, DC, these groups have guided and defined American environmentalism over the past three decades.

By the late 1960s and early 1970s, the environment had become a hot political issue. Government officials from every political persuasion claimed to be in favor of protecting the environment. On January 1, 1970, Republican President Richard M. Nixon signed the National Environmental Policy Act (NEPA). The act, among other things, required detailed environmental impact statements for all major federal actions and established the Council on Environmental Quality (CEQ) to advise the president and Congress on environmental matters (Vig and Kraft 1997). In addition, President Nixon heralded a national commitment to a healthier environment by stating that "the 1970s absolutely must be the years when America pays its debt to the past by reclaiming the purity of its air, its waters, and our living environment. It is literally now or never!" (Shabecoff 1993, 112).

The new environmental leadership took advantage of the environment's status on the systemic agenda to mobilize millions of concerned advocates. A 1970 Gallup poll reported that 53 percent of Americans viewed reduction of air and water pollution as a national priority, up from 17 percent in 1965. By the 1990s, over 80 percent of Americans considered themselves "environmentalists" (Dunlap 1995). This widespread public support was accompanied by the creation of new federal agencies, most notably the Environmental Protection Agency (EPA). The widespread public concern for the environment also encouraged government to take assertive legislative action to prevent environmental degradation. Environmental issues became a permanent fixture on the governmental agenda, a status reinforced by the creation of an environmental bureaucracy and congressional committees charged with oversight of environmental matters (Eisner, et al, 2000).

The political appeal of the environmental issues drove policymakers to support tough new measures readily, even when the full impact and costs of new policies where unknown. As a result, the decade of the 1970s saw many federal legislative victories for the environmental movement. Congress passed the Clean Air Act Amendments of 1970, the Federal Water Pollution Control Act Amendments and the Federal Environmental Pesticide Control Act of 1972, the Endangered Species Act of 1973, the Safe Drinking Water Act of 1974, the Toxic Substances Control Act and the Resource Conservation and Recovery Act of 1976, the Federal Water Pollution Control Act Amendments and the Surface Mining Control and Reclamation Act of 1977. In agenda setting language, the issue enjoyed near permanent status on the systemic, government, and decision agendas. To cyclical theorists the new environmentalism was the logical reaction to post-war decades of government backed industrialization (Truman 1951; Schlesinger 1986; McFarland 1991). If the new environmentalism was a cyclical phenomenon, the question was how long would it be before there was a counter-reaction.

Environmental Derailment, Rejuvenation, and Stagnation

Events in the political stream supplied the impetus for a challenge to the preeminence of environmental matters on the government agenda. The election of Republican Ronald Reagan as president, a self proclaimed "sagebrush rebel," ushered in the property rights movement. Reagan led an administration determined to deregulate, defund, and disband the environmental protection regime (and most regulation) (Mitchell 1984; Vig and Kraft 1997). When the initial Reagan legislative strategy failed, due to continued congressional support of environmental regulation, the president pursued an administrative route (Short 1989). The Reagan administration pursued reductions in staffing, research, and enforcement activities under the leadership of EPA administrator Anne Gorsuch and Secretary of Interior James Watt. The Reagan administration's environmental policies were the highest profile counter-reaction to the earlier successes of the environmental movement, but they were not the only counter-movement.

The attempt by the Reagan administration to rollback environmental regulation actually revived the issue on the public and congressional agendas. If environmental issues had been bumped from the public and congressional agendas by the sluggish economy, high inflation, the series of energy crises, and the Iranian hostage crisis (Dunlap 1987; Harris 1989), Reagan's lax enforcement of pollution laws and pro-development resource policies created political issues around which national and grassroots environmental groups could organize. Public concern with the health and environmental risks brought on by an industrial society and by the threats to ecological stability once again came to the fore. Membership in, and the revenue of, environmental organizations enjoyed a renaissance in the 1980s (see Bosso 1997). The marked increase in membership and revenues suggested that environmental issues enjoyed a permanent place on the systemic and government agendas (Hays 1987).

Reflecting this seemingly permanent agenda status, Congress continued to pursue environmental protection on the decision agenda throughout the Reagan administration. Among the most notable legislation enacted into law during this period were the Resource Conservation Act of 1984, the Superfund Amendments and Reauthorization Act of 1986, the Safe Drinking Water Act of 1986, and the Clean Air Act of 1987.

The election of Reagan's vice president, George Bush, as president in 1988 marked the ascension of a self proclaimed "environmental president" (Bosso 1997). The Bush administration had little choice in responding to the rejuvenated and widespread public concern for the environment. The 1986 accident at the Chernobyl nuclear power plant in the Soviet Union; a near repeat of the Bhopal chemical spill (1987) at a Union Carbide plant in Institute, West Virginia in 1988; the massive oil spill following the grounding of the *Exxon Valdez* in Prince William Sound; and the increasing evidence of global warming, kept environmental protection in the public eye (Eisner, Worsham and Ringquist 2000, 160-163). Bush's first two years in office reflected the dominance of environmental issues on the public agenda, culminating in the passage of the 1990 Clean Air Act Amendments (CAA). Soon after, however, Bush embarked on a policy course reminiscent of the Reagan administration, using the Council on Competitiveness to attack existing environmental regulation. A presidential commission backed clear-cutting in federal forests, emission limits were relaxed for toxic pollutants, and several parts of the CAA were weakened. The Council on Competitiveness, headed by Vice President Dan Quayle, met in closed session with industry actors effected by regulation. As such, it granted the property rights advocates an institutional foothold in the Bush administration (Eisner, Worsham and Ringquist 2000).

With respect to property rights, perhaps the most important event occurring during the Bush administration concerned wetlands. During his tenure as president, the EPA, under then-administrator William Reilly, issued a new wetlands delineation manual in 1989. The new manual broadened the definition of "navigable waters" and redefined lands that held water for short periods of time each year as "wetlands." This change led to a doubling in the amount of land over which the federal government exercised control (from 100 to 200 million acres). More importantly, over 75 percent of the new "wetlands" were privately owned (Marzulla 1995). The ultimate consequence of the redefinition was the expansion of federal control over property rights under the Clean Water Act. Realizing the error of its ways, the Bush administration proposed redefining wetlands in such a way as to undo the doubling accomplished by Reilly (Huth 1992).

The election of President Bill Clinton and Vice President Al Gore in 1992 brought a sense of euphoria to the environmental movement. In addition to the strong environmental stance in the Democratic platform, environmentalists were bolstered by Al Gore's reputation as the leading environmentalist in the Senate and his best selling book *Earth in the Balance*. Their expectations were satisfied by Clinton's decisive moves early in his first term. One of Clinton's first acts was to abolish Quayle's Council on Competitiveness and replace it with the Office of Environmental Protection (which was later folded into the Council for Environmental Quality) headed by Gore's protégé Kathleen McGinty. Clinton also issued executive orders requiring consideration of environmental justice and mandating pollution prevention and waste reduction throughout the federal government (Vig 1997).

Despite these and other innovations in environmental policy and administration, some argue that Clinton's environmental leadership was weak at best (Wicker 1994; Dowie 1995). In explanation, some argue that the president failed to effectively communicate his environmental policies to the public (Jones 1995). Others argue events in the political stream, in the form of the Republican congressional victories in 1994, explain the middling record. The GOP takeover of Congress ushered in a new Republican leadership largely unsympathetic to most of the environmental legislation of the previous two decades (Rosenbaum 1998). The 1994 elections initiated six years of warfare between the congressional critics of existing environmental legislation and their property rights allies on one side and environmentalists, their congressional allies, and the Clinton White House, on the other.

The Institutionalization of Environmentalism

Since 1970, Congress has passed a myriad of environmental laws that, when taken as a whole, create a complex regulatory web that includes restrictions on property use. The Clean Air Act (CAA), originally passed in 1970, amended in 1971, 1973, 1974, 1976, 1977, and significantly overhauled in 1990, regulates the emission of pollutants into the atmosphere {42 U.S.C., Section 7401-7671q (1988 & Supp. 1991)}. It requires "major sources" of air pollution to obtain permits designating their allowable amount of emissions. The CAA is primarily implemented through state legislation that must be submitted for federal review in the form of a State Implementation Plan (SIP). In the case where a state fails to submit a satisfactory SIP, the federal government may impose a Federal Implementation Plan as well as subject the state to sanctions, such as a cut-off of highway construction funds or a limit on its allowable emissions. The CAA's effect on the use of private property is tangential for most citizens in that it really only influences the siting and activities of commercial enterprises that produce emissions or the manufacturers of pollution producing equipment (Marzulla 1995).

The Clean Water Act (CWA) of 1972 regulates the discharge of pollutants into the nation's waterways {33 U.S.C., pgs.,401-26p, 441-54 (1988)}. Similar to Clean Air, the Clean Water Act is implemented through state permitting programs called the National Pollution Discharge Elimination System (NPDES). Yet, there is no State Implementation Plan. Rather, the federal government determines the water quality standards the state must achieve. Therefore, just as the Clean Air Act restricts the uses of private land by requiring permits for new and expanding sources of air emissions, the Clean Water Act limits land use where there is any significant discharge of pollutants into the water. Given the variety of activities that can result in such discharges, from manufacturing to farming, the CWA effects a more varied population than does the CAA.

Section 404 of the Clean Water Act imposes a more direct impact on the rights of some property owners. Section 404 grants the federal government authority over approximately 100 million acres of wetlands, a large portion of which is in private hands. The private owner of a wetland is prohibited from altering the property, and will rarely receive any compensation from the government for so doing. Despite this intrusion of property rights, the property owner is still expected to pay property taxes on the land, and on the passing of the land to heirs, they may pay inheritance taxes based on the fair market value before the effects of the regulatory restriction (Ceplo 1995).

The Endangered Species Act (ESA) passed in 1973, and amended in 1976, 1977, 1978, 1980, 1982, and 1988, is a comprehensive piece of legislation aimed at preserving endangered species {16 U.S.C., p.1533-44 (1988)}. Section 9 of the ESA bears the greatest consequences for property owners. It prohibits the "taking" of any species of animal or plant listed by the U.S. Fish and Wildlife Service (for terrestrial species) and National Marine Fisheries Service (for marine species) as endangered. The term "take" is defined in Section 3 as "to harass, harm, pursue, hunt, shoot, wound, kill, trap, capture, collect, or to attempt to engage in any such conduct." The Fish and Wildlife Service (FWS) has defined "harm" and "harass" as any activity that adversely modifies habitat, therefore harming or injuring just one member of a listed species (50 C.F.R., Section 17.3 1992). Typically, it is the "harm and harass" provision that restricts property owners in cases involving endangered species.

The endangered species list includes nearly 1,400 species and subspecies, including their habitat. Congress originally funded the Fish and Wildlife Service (FWS) to buy sensitive habitat from private owners, and from 1966 to 1989 it purchased 735,396 acres of private land for habitat and other protective purposes (Dunlap 1988). The Fish and Wildlife Service now uses the ESA to engage in regulatory takings. According to its interpretation of the law, the FWS may prevent landowners from developing, harvesting timber, farming or any other activity in order to protect resident species on the land (Welch 1995). Violaters of Section 9 of the ESA may be subject to a civil fine up to $25,000 for each violation and a criminal penalty up to $50,000 and/or imprisonment up to one year {16 U.S.C., p.1540 (1988)}.

State environmental regulations add another layer of rules to the regulatory web. A number of federal statutes are written to create a minimum, or "floor," for state environmental protection in the effort to discourage a state from becoming a "pollution haven" where industry may flee to avoid environmental regulation. However, many federal laws allow the states a good deal of flexibility in determining how they will achieve compliance with the federal requirements. States are allowed to go beyond the minimum federal requirements and adopt more stringent regulations. For example, California, New York, and Colorado have adopted more stingent air pollution regulations (Marzulla 1995). Federal regulations also guide programs for controlling water pollution, wetlands, non-municipal drinking water supplies, underground injection, and other hazardous waste treatment or disposal programs.

States take the lead in a number of other environmental areas. State regulators oversee programs concerning mineland bonding and reclamation, the application of agricultural chemicals, and the protection of groundwater (Rabe 1997). Also, states often augment federal regulations when they want to regulate certain activities not covered in the federal law. This has been evidenced through state "mini-superfunds," requirements within State Environmental Protection Acts (SEPA), recycling laws, labeling rules, and "community right-to-know" requirements (Rosenbaum 1998). State and local governments are primarily responsible for zoning and land use restrictions on private property (Smith 1995). Furthermore, these land use regulations have expanded to include historic preservation, battlefield protection, scenic designations, setbacks along waterways and streams, farmland protection, establishment of "greenways," buffer zones, designation of parks and preserves, and restrictions on natural resource development. Finally, state and local governments often use incentive/disincentive policies, such as licensing and permitting schemes, and tax incentives, to encourage or discourage certain economic activities that affect the environment (Hoerner 1995).

Enforcing the Rules: The "Three Ls" of the Environmental Movement

The environmental movement today is dominated by a handful of large, nationally based groups headquartered in Washington D.C., that are staffed by professionals drawn from fields ranging from law to business administration.

Their approach to protecting the environment can be summed up as the three L's—legislation, lobbying, and litigation. The legislative approach focuses attention on Congress and the authorization or reauthorization of environmental regulation. It also means maintaining the support of millions of voters, regardless of political ideology, to maintain the public agenda status of environmental issues. Leaders of the environmental movement make constant reference to the "green" voting block to remind members of Congress about the potential pitfalls of crossing the movement come election time.

In 1969 there were only two registered environmental lobbyists in Washington, DC. By 1985, when the environmental lobby was proclaimed "the most effective lobby in Washington," there were eighty-eight registered environmental lobbyists (Mitchell, Mertig, Dunlap 1985, 228). The number approached one hundred in 1990, as lobbying became increasingly congressional in focus. Lobbying finds environmentalists testifying at hearings, meeting with legislators, buttonholing executive branch personnel—in short, making sure no decision-maker goes unapproached. Over time this has become an increasingly DC centered activity, although the local chapters of the various national groups also work state houses on a regular basis.

The litigation strategy involves using the courts to force the federal government, and the EPA in particular, to enforce the law. Citizens and interest groups use litigation to protect legislative gains and to settle on implementation guidelines in line with the goals of the movement. In the

1970s, the dockets of the courts were filled with cases brought by the Environmental Defense Fund (EDF), the Natural Resource Defense Council (NRDC), the National Wildlife Federation (NWF), and the Sierra Club Legal Defense Fund (SCLDF) against violators of state and federal laws.

The litigation approach was successful through the mid-1980s, when the success rate began to decline. The answer as to why this decline occurred is simple. By 1992, more than half of the federal district and appellate justices were Reagan and Bush appointees. Most were hostile to federal regulation and to the use of the courts by private citizens to redress policy grievances (Bork 1989). More and more these judges issued rulings that required the consideration of cost-benefit criteria in enforcing health, safety, and environmental regulation. The courts increasingly challenged federal agencies' authority to impose regulations, as well as their implementation of regulations. They also began ruling that plaintiffs that once had standing in their courts no longer enjoyed that right. In short, the courts became a less hospitable venue for the environmental movement as the 1990s unfolded.

The environmental movement's "Three L's" strategy relied heavily on the ability of national level institutions to write and enforce environmental policy. This was both its strength and its weaknesses (Dowie 1995; Bosso 1997). The national level focus and strategy alienated some grassroots supporters, as well as those previously neutral on the issue, opening the door for the property rights movement to co-opt many who might otherwise be natural allies of the environmentalists (Bosso 1997). The ultimate irony is that given our political system, environmentalists had to develop a professional organization capable of doing battle with entrenched industrial interests if it was to survive. In order to pursue complex lawsuits in the federal courts and provide financial and technical assistance to activists in an array of state and local venues, the movement had to go nationwide. But in going nationwide, and enjoying such success, it set itself up for a counterrevolution.

Igniting Antagonism

Taken together, this array of federal, state, and local regulation form a maze of rules and restrictions that apply to a wide variety of economic activities. Indeed, it is little wonder that individuals may become frustrated by an inability to understand and comply with the variety of rules and regulations that constitute the "regulatory thicket" of environmental protection. More important, business resents such regulation as raising the cost of doing business. Economic actors long accustomed to doing as they please resent health and safety regulation as interference and micro-management. The genius of the property rights movement is that major industry players channeled and used public frustration to create a movement that challenged the preeminence of environmental beliefs (Dowie 1995; Switzer 1997).

The environmental regulations of the 1970s serve as the first stimulus of the property rights movement. With the implementation of the new environmental laws, a good deal of industry faced regulators with the power to restrict their use of productive assets. Industry felt it was being singled out to bear the burden of providing a public good. Worse still, while regulators were willing to adapt the implementation of some laws, so as to ease the burden of regulation, environmental groups would not let them. Time after time the EPA was taken to court when it attempted to compromise with industry. Externalities like oil spills, burning rivers, toxic waste dumps, and polluted skies evoked little public, or environmentalist, sympathy. Since polluting industries could do little on their own to achieve regulatory relief, the solution was to widen the scope of the conflict.

Initially, business interests were slow to react to the legislative initiatives proposed by the environmental movement (Hayes 1987). As industry groups came to realize the financial stake in the environmental debate, with cost estimates ranging in the hundreds of billions, they organized (Carlin, Scodari, Garner 1992). Because the stakes were so high, the industrial lobby—represented by the extractive resource industries, chemical manufacturers, the nuclear power industry, and automakers—had plenty of incentive to mobilize. Given their long experience in working the halls of Congress, the bulk of their efforts were directed at lobbying against future legislation and working to weaken legislation already in the pipeline. In addition, resources were also put into efforts to alter the implementation of existing environmental regulations, which meant working at the grassroots (Mann 1990).

If the economic consequences of much of the initial environmental regulation were undetermined in the early 1970s, the actions taken by President Carter in the later part of the decade regarding public lands left little doubt as to their effect. The Carter administration converted millions of acres of federal lands under the supervision of the Bureau of Land Management (BLM) into federal wilderness areas, national parks, and wildlife refuges. This more than doubled the size of the National Wildlife Refuge System and added five million miles of rivers to the National Wild and Scenic River System, a fourfold increase in four years. While property rights advocates attacked this move as yet another intrusion by beltway insiders on matters best left to local management, and used the issue of grazing permits to illustrate their point, in reality the refuge status also ruled out mining and oil exploration on public lands—a policy change that aroused the ire of the multinational minerals industry.

The "Sagebrush Rebellion" was a movement of western agriculture and mineral interests, joined and funded by multinationals involved in extractive mineral industries, that challenged the basis and purpose of environmental regulation. In its most radical moment it argued that the federal government had a trust obligation to dispose of public lands. During calmer periods it simply asked for the continuation of grazing and mineral leases that had served as the backbone of public lands management since the acquisition of the western United States. One theme remained constant, westerners were hostile toward the federal government's opposition to the pace of resource development in their region. Large leaseholders argued that the only way to gain control of the land and its resources was to deed federal land over to the states and then have the states sell it off (cheaply of course) to private interests (Dowie 1995). This approach to resource management promised huge profits for those lucky enough to become the private owners of western acreage (Salisbury 1981).

The Sagebrush Rebellion was not simply a multinational ruse. A variety of ordinary people dependent upon federal land for their livelihoods—farmers, ranchers, foresters, miners, and "inholders" (those with property bordering or surrounded by federal land)—began to organize against federal government policies that increasingly eroded their ability to earn a living. Trade associations representing each of these interests, such as the National Cattleman's Association, emerged to fight specific features of the new environmental regulation. True, it was organizations funded by the multinationals, such as the Center for the Defense of Free Enterprise (CDFE), that brought the groups together to form a common network. Still, there was genuine dissatisfaction at the grassroots.

Yet, the response from the mainstream environmental groups was non-existent. Instead of addressing the ultimate victims of the federal land acquisitions (i.e., the small landowners and ranchers), they concentrated on keeping regulators honest. As a result, they failed to acknowledge the grievances of their grassroots opposition and missed the opportunity to forge some cooperative allegiances with their antagonists (Dowie 1995). This mistake came back to haunt them when the "Sagebrush Rebellion" morphed into the "Wise Use" movement.

Always the master of spin, the industrial interests who put together the Wise Use "movement" appropriated their name from one of the leading philosophers of American conservation, Gilford Pinchot. As founder of the Society of American Foresters and the first chief of the United States Forest Service, Pinchot argued that "[c]onservation means the *wise use* of the earth and its resources for the lasting good of men" (Pinchot 1947, 505). There is some irony in that his philosophy of sustainable management and multiple use of natural resources provides the philosophical underpinnings for a focused effort to oppose environmentalism and conservation.

The Wise Use "movement" was the creation of two individuals—Ron Arnold and Alan Gottlieb. Ron Arnold can make the curious claim of having been a member of the Sierra Club. His membership ended when he formed his own graphics company and took on timber interests as his clients. Arnold is associated with a variety of right-wing causes, including his own publishing house (with Gottlieb as a partner). As the executive director of the Center for the Defense of Free Enterprise (CDFE), he promotes these causes and declares himself an irrefutable adversary of the environmental movement, whose aim, in his own words, is to "destroy the environmental movement once and for all!" (Dowie 1995, 93). Alan Gottlieb, a conservative fundraiser who specializes in forming "citizen groups" to pursue rightwing causes, teamed with Arnold to launch the new opposition movement after a Multiple Use Strategy Conference sponsored by the CDFE in August, 1988. Using their own publishing house, they produced *The Wise Use Agenda* in 1989 (Gottleib 1989; Switzer 1997, 200). Always the masters of spin, Gottlieb and Arnold claimed a membership of thousands and issued the *Agenda* as their manifesto. The *Agenda* reads like a developers' wish list, advocating the abandonment of the ESA, increased logging and mineral exploration on public lands, and turning over Park Service responsibilities to private firms.

While Arnold and Gottlieb speak in terms of a vast movement of the disgruntled, the reality is less dramatic and more complex. The Wise Use movement is not so much a movement, as it is a loose collection of organizations, each of which represents groups opposed to some facet of environmental regulation or conservation (Switzer 1997, 200-205). Some of the umbrella groups associated with Wise Use appear to be classic efforts at astro-turf lobbying. For example, the Western States Public Lands Coalition, was a creation of the mining industry. The WSPLC itself created an interest group, People for the West!, to act as a front for mining industry interests when Congress attempted to revise the 1872 mining laws (Byrnes 1992). Others, like the Blue Ribbon Coalition, are a loose knit group of outdoor recreation enthusiasts dedicated "to the preservation of all forms of off-road recreation in an environmentally responsible manner" (Switzer 1997, 201). The coalition produces a monthly newsletter to notify subscribers of any federal or state level laws and regulations that impact off-road recreation. While Arnold and Gottlieb claim to speak for all through their positions with the CFDFE, the reality is more chaotic. Still, the Wise Use movement, with the CDFE at its helm, sought to redefine the terms of the environmental policy debate, while also widening the scope of the conflict.

The problem when studying Wise Use is that it is often difficult to separate fact from fiction. Arnold and Gottlieb are quick to latch onto local opposition to specific elements of environmental and conservation regulation as part of their movement. Using the internet and desk-top publications, they are their own best cheerleaders. At the same time, they do provide points of contact and an electronic town hall that brings together what otherwise would be isolated local groups or individuals. While the opposition may begin as local, Wise Use offers it "fifteen minutes of (national) fame" via their publicity network. For example, the Shasta Alliance for Resources and Environment (SHARE) was created in 1986 by the Greater Redding, California, Chamber of Commerce, with help from the CDFE. It touted itself as an "independent committee" focusing on resource management policies of northern California (Alliance for Environment and Resources 1998). In reality, the alliance sought an end to logging restrictions that protected much of California's old growth redwood forests—restrictions that local timber interests resented.

While the Wise Use movement portrayed itself as a grass roots reaction to beltway interference, in reality the bulk of its funding and resources comes from large corporations whose economic interests are threatened by regulation. Companies such as Exxon, Louisiana Pacific, Boise Cascade, Champion Paper, and MCI fund the movement directly, or indirectly through foundations set up for that purpose (O'Keefe and Daley 1993). Still, the movement's message does appeal to small landowners who are repeatedly told that the federal government and the environmentalists are conspiring to steal their land (Brick 1995). Undoubtedly, Wise Use rhetoric has attracted members by redefining environmental issues in economic and property rights terms. In the words of David Helvarg, who spent three years studying Ron Arnold, Alan Gottlieb, and their followers, the Wise Use Movement is "a backlash...a large and well organized backlash" against environmentalism (Helvarg 1994, 137).

Redefining the Issue: The Right to Property

In 1972, the Supreme Court noted: "In fact, a fundamental interdependence exists between the personal right to liberty and the personal right to property. Neither would have meaning without the other" {*Lynch v. Household Finance Corporation*, 405 U.S. 538, 552 (1972)}. The Property Rights movement takes this opinion as gospel, viewing conservation and environmental regulation as an attack on liberty (Helvarg 1994). Nancie Marzulla, president and founder of Defenders of Property Rights, argues that "the property rights battle has now become a fight for freedom and individual rights, with property recognized as more than just land" (Marzulla 1995). On one extreme, adherents accuse the environmental movement of believing the world would be a better place without it human inhabitants, favoring Orwellian analogies to "Big Brother" when speaking of the EPA and the Endangered Species Act (Knox 1993). According to Michael Wasylik of the Defenders of Property Rights: "the entire property rights movement is a reaction to government regulations as a whole, including environmental protection, historical protection, and the attitude that government could solve all problems (Wasylik 1999). When they do mention conservation or environmental protection, it is to make the argument that only the exclusive ownership of property provides effective, long-term incentives required to conserve resources and minimize pollution (Marzulla 1995).

The taking movement claims its roots are embedded in that part of the Fifth Amendment to the U.S. Constitution that states, "nor shall private property be taken for public use, without just compensation." This legal principle is referred to as the "taking clause" and protects the property owner from governmental condemnation or seizure without "just compensation." Note that nothing prohibits the taking of private property for public purposes. Rather, the Constitution simply requires compensation. Ruling in *Armstrong v. U.S.*, the Supreme Court ruled that the purpose of the taking clause was "to bar government from forcing some people to bear the public burdens which, in all fairness and justice, should be borne by the public as a whole" {364 U.S. 40 (1960)}.

The guarantee contained in the taking clause was extended to the states by the Fourteenth's Amendment's due process clause, which states, "nor shall any state deprive any person of life, liberty, or property, without the due process of law." With respect to public land use decisions, due process requirements usually include the notification of governmental action and the opportunity for a formal hearing (Coyle 1993). The due process clause protects individuals from arbitrary and unreasonable State government action, but offers no guarantee that the property owner will retain unlimited rights to the use of land.

Despite the constitutional guarantees regarding the right to property, government reserves the right to infringe upon private property rights in select instances. Through its "police power," government has the right to regulate the use of private property for the protection of public health, safety, and general welfare. With respect to land use, zoning and nuisance laws are the most common use of the police power. The Supreme Court has upheld the principle of zoning, ruling that it does not constitute a governmental taking in *Village of Euclid v. Ambler Reality Co.* {272 U.S. 365, 395 (1926)}, and in *Nectow v. City of Cambridge* {277 U.S. 183, 187 (1928)}. Similarly, the Supreme Court has consistently ruled that the right to property does not include the right to injure or endanger the public, that is to create a nuisance, and that owners that do so must expect to "suffer regulation without compensation" (Plotkin 1987, 68).

The most dramatic fashion in which government infringes on the right to property is through the power of eminent domain. This action typically involves the physical transfer of the property to the government itself or a third party, such as a public utility. Through eminent domain the government acquires title to the property for some public purpose, such as the construction of electrical transmission lines, roads, and similar. Eminent domain appears to be the most direct use of the government's powers to infringe on property rights in that it involves confiscation, albeit with compensation. At issue in all such cases is the amount of compensation due. The taking movement fastened onto this question, as well as the definition of what constitutes a taking, in fashioning an attack on environmental regulation.

According to property rights advocates, a regulatory taking is said to occur whenever there has been a diminution in the market value of land caused by government action (Fellows 1996). A regulatory taking is different from an outright seizure, such as that which occurs through government exercising the power of eminent domain. A regulatory taking does not entail a transfer of title, and often times only a portion of the property is effected. A regulatory taking differs from a land use restriction via zoning when the regulation provides a "reasonable use over a reasonable period of time" as measured by a comprehensive plan (Freilich and Garvin 1993).

A regulatory taking is different from any action resulting from government's police power and its right of eminent domain. Most importantly, a regulatory taking is not a categorical condemnation of property by the government. A regulatory taking generally involves only a partial taking. That is, it usually results in the elimination of only a fraction of the property value, even though the restriction applies to the property as a whole. Yet, a regulatory taking can result in the loss of the entire value of the property. A regulatory taking also applies when only part of the property is restricted, such as when the government mandates an easement to use the property as a *quid pro quo* with the owner.

The issues surrounding regulatory taking have become the topics for heated debate, both in government and society. This is no surprise given the legal and economic implications involved. The call for action to resolve this issue is backed by national extractive resource associations like the American Mining Congress and the American Petroleum Institute, in conjunction with the American Farm Bureau and the National Association of Realtors, as well as local land owners and recreation enthusiasts. It is the debate over what constitutes a taking, and just compensation, that preoccupies those interested in setting the property rights agenda. The debate has occurred in multiple venues over the past three decades. Property owners traditionally turned to the courts in an attempt to set the agenda, a subject to which we now turn.

CHAPTER FOUR

The Courts as a Venue

The judicial system is an important venue for those interested in redefining an issue. To date the courts have played a significant, albeit limited, role in deciding what constitutes a taking and fashioning remedies for same. What they have not done is questioned the constitutional basis of takings, which from the view of some, makes them a less than ideal venue for settling the issue. Still, the courts have served as something more than a simple arbiter between the various factions. Why this is so is obvious on one level, while these are questions of law and interpretation of the law, questions that demand arbitration, they are more than that. They are also questions regarding the purpose of government, the right of property, and the distribution of power in the polity—issues from which the court rarely shies away.

Our survey of the court as an alternative venue for issue definition is far from definitive. Rather, our purpose is to trace how the discussion of takings has evolved over time. As such, we limit ourselves to a review of Supreme Court cases, in the naïve belief that a decision in that forum serves as some type of authoritative definition of the issue. Nothing, of course, could be further from the truth (as the following makes clear).

The evolution of property rights in the Court

Historically, the courts reading of property rights has favored capital (Orren 1991; Brisbin 1993). And, as many of the following cases illustrate, it was industry that used the courts to try to limit the power of government to regulate their use of property. Interestingly, the early efforts were rebuffed by the courts. In *Mugler v. Kansas* {123 U.S. 623 (1887)} and *Hadacheck v. Sebastian* {239 U.S. 394 (1915)}, the Supreme Court declined to find taking for regulations that served significant public purposes despite a significant impact on property value.

Shortly after those rulings the Court's 1922 decision in *Pennsylvania Coal v. Mahon* {260 U.S. 393 (1922)} established for the first time that the mere regulation of property, even for valid purposes, might constitute a taking if the court finds the regulation's costs to the property owner to be excessive. The *Pennsylvania Coal* case involved the legitimacy of Pennsylvania's Kohler Act, prohibiting mining that caused subsidence under any house, street, or public building. In defending the regulation, Pennsylvania argued that the new law was a legitimate exercise of its police power required to protect public health and safety and, therefore, immune to a taking challenge. The problem, from the vantage of the coal industry, was that they had sold the surface rights to much of the land they once held outright to individuals. The sales had been made with the understanding that the coal companies retained the mineral rights to the property, forcing buyers to waive any right to future claims against the company for subsidence damages. The mining industry argued that the regulation constituted a taking of private property, in that by preventing it from mining the seams of coal likely to produce subsidence, the state was taking its property.

The Court sided with the coal industry, ruling that despite the law's intention it violated the Fourteenth Amendment's due process guarantees and that the state must buy the company's interest in order to achieve its goal constitutionally. This marked the first time the Court recognized that a regulation could result in an unconstitutional taking and require compensation - regardless of whether the government physically occupied or assumed title to the property. In expressing the Court's opinion of when a regulation constitutes a taking, Justice Oliver Wendell Holmes wrote, "While property may be regulated to a certain extent, if the regulation goes too far, it will be recognized as a taking" {260 U.S. 393, p.415 (1922)}. The Court did not elaborate on how to make future determinations of what constituted "too far," leaving the determination to be decided in future challenges. In the end the Court created an ambiguous "too far" standard that did little to clearly delimit when a regulatory taking had occurred. Still, the Court signaled both public and private actors that some police powers might constitute a taking, requiring redress. Despite the Court's recognition of a regulatory taking in *Pennsylvania Coal*, it did not invalidate another government action as a regulatory taking for the next sixty years. Instead, in a number of cases the Court upheld land use restrictions on property use despite substantial economic loss.

It was not until 1978, in *Pennsylvania Central Transportation Company v. New York* {438 U.S. 104 (1978)}, that the Court attempted to refine the criteria to be used in determining when a compensable taking had occurred. The Court enunciated three criteria to be considered in making such a determination: the character of the government action; the economic impact of the action on the claimant; and, the extent to which the action interfered with the investment-backed expectations of the claimant (Marzulla 1988, 10255).

The *Penn Central* case involved the 1965 New York City Landmarks Preservation Act passed in an effort to protect historic buildings and districts. In 1968, a joint proposal by Penn Central and UGI Properties was submitted to the Commission charged with enforcing the act. The proposal called for building a fifty-five-story office building in the airspace over Grand Central Terminal, which had been designated a historical landmark in 1967. The Commission denied the permit, and Penn Central and UGI Properties filed suit claiming that the application of the Landmarks Preservation Law constituted a taking of their property without just compensation.

In deciding in favor of the City, the Court ruled that the restriction prohibiting developing the airspace above the terminal constituted only one property right. The owners were still able to utilize the property as a terminal, which in the Court's opinion, offered a reasonable investment return. Also, the Court determined that the regulation was not arbitrarily applied, but affected other property owners as well, who were similarly burdened and benefited by the law.

A decade passed before another significant taking case appeared before the Supreme Court. In 1987 the Supreme Court decided three taking cases - *Keystone Bituminous Coal Association v. DeBenedictus* {480 U.S. 470 (1987)}, *First English Evangelical Lutheran Church of Glendale v. County of Los Angeles* {482 U.S. 304 (1987)}, and *Nollan v. California Coastal Commission* {483 U.S. 825 (1987)}. Also, in 1988 the Court rendered a crucial decision in *Agins v. City of Tiburon* {447 U.S. 255 (1988)} with regards to regulatory taking. Despite the new conservative Court's willingness to hear the taking challenges, the rulings did not define precisely what constitutes a regulatory taking. The brief review of these cases will clarify this point.

The first case, *Keystone Bituminous Coal Association v. DeBenedictus*, dealt with the traditional police power of state land use regulation. Pennsylvania passed the Bituminous Mine Conservation Act ("Subsidence Act") which prohibited bituminous coal mining that could lead to cave-ins, collapses, or subsidence that could damage public buildings, human dwellings, and cemeteries. The reported goal of the Act was to "guard the health, safety, and general welfare of the public." The Pennsylvania Department of Environmental Resources enforced the statute by regulation, one of which required the coal miners to leave 50 percent of the coal in place under the protected structures in order to prevent subsidence (480 U.S. 470, p.476-77, 1987)). An association of mining interests sought an injunction, on the grounds that the regulation resulted in the state effectively taking 27 million tons of coal (which equaled only 2 percent of the total coal seam) without compensation.

In upholding the legitimacy of the Subsidence Act, the Supreme Court cited the precedent set in *Pennsylvania Coal* that a regulation that goes "too far" would be considered a taking. Yet, it distinguished the case from its predecessor by concluding that there was not a sufficient diminution in property value to constitute a regulatory taking. In deciding the case, the Supreme Court reasoned that since the same person owned the "support estate" (matter below the surface) and either the surface estate or the mineral estate, that the support estate was only one "strand" in a larger "bundle" of property rights. The Court asserted that when determining whether governmental action constitutes a taking it should evaluate the impact of the regulation relative to the property as a whole. Since mining the 27 million tons of coal represented only one "strand" of property rights, the state's regulation was not excessive because it did not destroy the larger "bundle" of rights, which still included the right to mine coal profitably. Therefore, the Court ruled the Subsidence Act was not a taking because it advanced a legitimate public interest, it prevented a nuisance, and it still allowed the company an opportunity to make a profit.

In the second case, *First English Evangelical Lutheran Church of Glendale v. County of Los Angeles*, the court ruled for the first time that compensation was due for the loss of land value during the time a regulation went into effect and the time the Court subsequently struck down the ordinance as a regulatory taking. The facts of the case have the First English Evangelical Lutheran Church buying 21 acres of land in 1957 to use as a campground and recreation area. In 1978 a flood destroyed all the buildings on the grounds. In response to the disaster the County of Los Angeles banned all building and construction in flood control areas, which included the Church's land. Consequently, the Church filed a claim alleging that the ban denied all use of its land and, thus, was a governmental taking without compensation.

In deciding the case, the Court did not decide whether or not the regulation in question constituted a taking. Instead, it addressed the issue of remedies available after a taking has occurred. It agreed that the church was entitled to compensation for the period of time that the regulation denied all reasonable use of the property. The majority ruled that once private property has been taken, just compensation is required from the date the regulation affects the property until the date when the government either revokes or amends the regulation. The Court held that the invalidation of the regulation only limits that compensation by avoiding the continuation of the taking. However, invalidation alone does not constitute just compensation for the time the regulation remained in effect (Eisenberg 1988). Chief Justice Rehnquist stressed this point in declaring that "the constitution guarantees the compensation remedy when a taking occurs, regardless of the duration of the taking, or of subsequent governmental action intended to remedy the situation" (482 U.S. 304, p.321, 1987). The property rights movement may look at this ruling as a victory. It ensures that compensation will be paid to the landowner for losses incurred as a result of a regulatory taking, no matter how long the property owner was subject to the regulation.

It is worth reiterating that the *First English* case did not provide any guidance in determining when a regulatory taking occurs. Instead, it further established the guarantee of the compensation remedy when a governmental action is determined to be a taking. In making this point, Chief Justice Rehnquist repeated a well established resolution that government regulation of property rights can be a taking and concluded that after a regulation does effect a taking, the duration of that regulation is irrelevant to the requirement of compensation. He wrote, "the only difference between a permanent taking and a temporary taking is that the valuation of the compensation is less in the latter instance, because the government should only have to pay compensation for the time during which its regulatory taking was in effect" (482 U.S. 304, p.319, 1987).

In the third case, *Nollan v. California Coastal Commission*, the Court addressed the practice by local governments of requiring land or financial contributions by developers to help offset the cost of public facilities necessitated by their development. In this case, the Nollans owned a beachfront lot located between two public beaches. When the Nollans decided to build a new house on their lot, they applied for a permit from the California Coastal Commission as the law required. The Commission granted the permit on the condition that they set aside a strip of their property so that the public may move between the two beaches. The Commission defended the condition on the grounds that the new house would reduce the view of the beach from the street and prevent the public "psychologically" from realizing that a stretch of coastline existed nearby that they are able to access. The Nollans protested the condition, arguing that it amounted to an unconstitutional taking without compensation.

The Supreme Court ruled that the Commission violated the Taking Clause of the Fifth Amendment by requiring the property owners to convey an easement across their property before they could receive a permit to build their home. In writing its decision, the Court asserted that a development condition, or extraction, does not constitute a taking as long as it advances a legitimate governmental interest or is adopted in response to the specific needs created by the development. In other words, there must be an "essential nexus," or necessary connection, between the governmental mandate to the property owner and the public interest in order for the regulation not to amount to a taking. In the *Nollan* case, however, the Court found that there was an insufficient connection between the required extraction and the impact of the proposed development, suggesting that its real purpose was an attempt to obtain a public easement without providing compensation (Symons 1988; Blaesser et al. 1989).

In 1988, the Supreme Court decided the case of *Agins v. City of Tiburon* that involved an open-space zoning ordinance limiting the number of homes that could be built on a tract of land. In ruling against the property owner, the Court developed a two-part legal test, the "Agins test," to determine whether the government had gone too far and caused a regulatory taking. The Agins test determines that a regulatory taking occurs if the government's action either: exhibits an "impermissible use" of the government's police power; or denies the property owner "economically viable use" of the property (Fellows 1996).

If either of these conditions apply, then the government must compensate the owner for the loss in property value. In writing for the majority, Justice Lewis Powell clarified what "impermissible use" means by stating that the regulation or action must "substantially advance legitimate state interests" or else it would be considered an illegitimate use of the government's police power. Further elaborating on the impermissible use concept, the Court held that two subsidiary conditions must be met by the government. First, there must be an essential nexus between the regulation and the public interest. Second, there must be a reasonable relationship between the regulation and the public benefits. In other words, once the nexus between the regulation and the public interest is established, it must be proven that it is more than a loosely connected one. Having settled the *Agins* case under the first criterion of the Agins test, the Court failed to expand upon the second criterion which deals with "economically viable use." However, the opportunity to address this issue reappeared just five years later in a landmark property rights case.

In the 1992 case, *Lucas v. South Carolina Coastal Council* (112 S. Ct. 2886 (1992)}, the Supreme Court addressed the second criterion of the Agins test dealing with economically viable use. The case involved the state adoption of developmental restraints in coastal lands located within so-called "critical areas." In 1986, David Lucas (the plaintiff) purchased two residential lots on the Isle of Palms, a barrier island in Charleston County, South Carolina, for $975,000 with the intention to build single family homes on each of the lots. Two years later, South Carolina passed the Beachfront Management Act, which sought to preserve sensitive coastal areas by prohibiting construction within so-called "critical areas" of the shoreline. As a result, both of Lucas's lots were affected and he was effectively prohibited from building any structures on his property.

Lucas sued claiming that the Beachfront Act, despite its legitimate intention to protect South Carolina's beaches, denied him all economically viable uses of his property and, thus, was a taking that required compensation. The state argued that the "nuisance exception" to the taking clause allowed the regulation since it was aimed at both protecting the environment and preventing public hazards that might occur as a result of storm damage to the property's structures (Moffett 1996). The Supreme Court ruled in favor of Lucas, expressing that the state must rely on laws in force at the time the property was purchased to justify its developmental restraint. Also, the Court felt that the Act was an invalid exercise of the state's police powers to mitigate the potential harm to the public interest that Lucas's land might occasion (112 S. Ct. 2886, p.899, 1992).

The Court justified its taking decision based upon the "economically viable use" concept as well. The Court suggested that from the perspective of the landowner total deprivation of beneficial use was equivalent to a physical appropriation of the land. Therefore, "when the owner of real property has been called upon to sacrifice *all* economically beneficial uses in the name of the common good, ... he has suffered a taking" (112 S. Ct. 2886, p.2895, 1992). The court further noted that in such a case, the regulatory action is compensable without the usual inquiry into the public interest advanced by the regulation (Delaney 1993). The Court's ruling eventually led to the state's outright purchase of the land from Lucas for over $1.5 million.

The *Lucas* decision was a small victory for property owners in that it established the right to be compensated when a governmental regulation eliminates all economic use of one's land. It should be noted, however, that this represents an odd case, and even the Supreme Court acknowledged that a total economic loss was an "extraordinary circumstance" (Greenhouse 1992; Kenworthy and Downy 1992). On the other hand, environmentalists claimed the *Lucas* decision as victory for themselves because the requirement of compensation only applied to instances where there was total economic loss. This suggests that regulatory decisions reducing the value of land by anything less that one hundred percent were not necessarily compensable.

The Agins test was revisited in *Dolan v. City of Tigard* (114 S. Ct. 2309 1994). The Court again was asked to determine whether a government mandated extraction in return for a building permit constituted an "impermissible use" of the state's police power. In the *Dolan* case, the city of Tigard, Oregon granted Florence Dolan a permit to expand her hardware store and its parking lot on the condition that she dedicate land to improve a storm-drainage channel and a pedestrian / bicycle path. The city argued that these extractions were necessary to minimize flooding and relieve traffic congestion that might be caused by the additional traffic to her store. Together, the extractions would have taken ten percent of her 1.7 acre lot for public use, and there was to be no compensation for the public easements. Dolan sued, arguing that the city did not compensate her for effectively taking the property.

The Supreme Court ruled in favor of Dolan, citing their earlier decision in *Agins*. The Court acknowledged the validity of the city's goal to advance a legitimate state interest, following the first prong of the Agins test. Yet, the Court reiterated that the first prong of the Agins test had two subsidiary conditions, and both conditions had to be met for the government to accomplish an uncompensated taking. Therefore, once the essential nexus was established (a valid state interest involved), the state had to show that there was a reasonable relationship between the state interest and the government mandate to the property owner (Fellows 1996). The state failed in this second part, and the court ruled that the conditions set for the permit approval were disproportional to the anticipated impacts of development and, thus, constituted a violation of the Fifth Amendment's Taking Clause (Biskupic 1994; Greenhouse 1994).

In *Suitum v. Tahoe Regional Planning Agency* (117 S. Ct. 1659, 1997) the Court considered the question of ripeness, that is, when does a property owner have the right to bring a regulatory takings claim to court? Earlier rulings held that a final decision had to be made by the planning agency before a claim of a regulatory taking could be considered ripe for consideration (Lieberman 1997). The problem, from both the courts and citizens view, was in determining when an agency had made a final decision, since the latter often claimed that further administrative review was necessary before a decision could be considered final. The case before the Court concerned an undeveloped lot subject to land-use regulation administered by the Tahoe Regional Planning Agency. The agency had been charged with developing and implementing a plan that would prevent the further degradation of Lake Tahoe. It put in place a system by which property was scored as suitable or unsuitable for development. Recognizing the system would make some property subject to non-development, the agency was authorized to grant property owners transferable development rights (TDRs) that could be sold to property owners of other regulated parcels, enabling the latter to achieve a score which would allow development of their parcel (Lieberman 1997). Suitum had purchased her lot eight years prior to the enactment of the land use regulation, although her application to build on the lot was made nine years after the adoption of the regulations. Her application was denied by the agency after it was determined her parcel was in an area where all development was prohibited. Her appeal for relief to the agency's governing board was also denied, at which point she filed suit claiming the agency actions amounted to a taking without just compensation, in violation of the Fifth and Fourteenth Amendments.

The agency responded that the suit was not ripe, since Suitum had failed to determine the worth of her TDRs, in which case "the extent of her financial harm, if any, was unknown" (Lieberman 1997). The district court agreed with the agency, ruling that until Suitum tried to sell her TDRs it was impossible to tell if her investment expectations had been frustrated (Lieberman 1997). The Ninth Circuit upheld the lower court's dismissal on ripeness grounds using identical reasoning.

In deciding the case, the Supreme Court enunciated two independent criteria that had to be met before a takings claim could be considered ripe. First, "a plaintiff must demonstrate that ... [they have] received a final decision" so that the court can decide if the regulation "goes too far" and results in a taking under the Fifth Amendment. Second, the plaintiff must exhaust state provided procedures for seeking redress before making a claim based on Fifth Amendment protections, because "only takings without just compensation infringe on the Fifth Amendment" (117 S. Ct. 1659). Since the lower court had only addressed the first condition, the Supreme Court limited its focus to that issue. The Court found that a final decision had been made in Suitum's case and that she could proceed with her suit. Their reasoning was that because there was "no question here about how the regulations at issue [apply] to the particular land in question" the agency had in fact rendered a final judgement (Lieberman 1997). In this fashion the court established that if past practice indicated a particular judgement was likely, the agency action could be considered final.

Because it was not contested by either party, the matter of TDRs did not figure into the *Suitum* decision, although it was mentioned in the opinions. The question of TDRs split the court along a slightly different fault line than did the question of ripeness. Some of those in the property rights majority, as well as those in the minority, agree that TDRs have a role to play in determining the ripeness of a takings claim, as well as the economic consequences of land use regulation (Radford 1999). On the other side was Anton Scalia, who, in response to the suggestion in the majority opinion that the role of TDRs might have made a difference in the outcome, argued that the value of the TDRs involved the question of just compensation and not whether a taking had occurred.

Suitum was important in redefining ripeness, clearly signaling agencies that a pattern of action that constituted repeated denial of land use would be interpreted as final action. The discussion of TDRs also provided a potential opening for agencies to count them as compensation when the question of the economic impact of agency actions came under scrutiny.

In *City of Monterey v. Del Monte Dunes* {526 U.S. 687 (1999)} the Supreme Court reaffirmed its backing of property owners involved in land use disputes with municipal authorities. The case involved repeated denials by the City of Monterey for development of a 37.6 acre parcel of oceanfront property. The city planning commission denied the original application, but indicated it would approve a proposal that involved fewer residential units. Over the next five years four revised proposals were submitted, and each was denied. When the developers appeal was denied by the city council, which placed additional restrictions on their use of the parcel, the owners, Del Monte Dunes Corporation, sued the city in the District Court for the Northern District of California under 42 U.S.C. 1983, arguing the denial of the final proposal was a violation of the Due Process and Equal Protection Clauses of the Fourteenth Amendment an unconstitutional regulatory taking. The trial court submitted the takings and equal protection claims to a jury, which awarded Del Monte Dunes 1.45 million dollars in damages. The Ninth Circuit affirmed the decision, as did the Supreme Court in a 5-4 decision (Harvard 1999).

The Court identified three issues suitable for review. First, were the landowner's claims properly submitted to a jury? Second, was the action by the Court of Appeals that allowed the jury to consider the reasonableness of the city's land use decision permissible? Third, did the Court of Appeals err in applying the rough proportionality standard of *Dolan* to the case?

The Court noted that while the court of appeals had discussed the *Dolan* standard in the decision affirming the jury verdict, the instructions to the jury did not require, nor did they mention, rough-proportionality criteria (Stedfast 1999). The Court concluded that the standard did not apply and need not to have been discussed in the Appeals Court decision. Indeed, the Court noted that "we have not extended the rough-proportionality test of *Dolan* beyond the special context of exactions—land-use decisions conditioning approval of development on the dedication of property to public use" {526 U.S. 687 (1999) p1635}. The Court reiterated that the *Dolan* standard was meant to ensure demands placed on property owners were roughly proportional to the anticipated public impact of development. In so doing, the Court appeared to recognize the public interest effected by private development, and government actors' authority to protect the public, within limits.

That said, the Courts decision on the first two questions clearly favored property owners. In deciding that the property owner's damage claims were properly submitted to the jury, the Court drew on the Seventh Amendment right to a jury trial in matters of common law. While the Court observed there was no such right inherent in Section 1983 cases per se, cases that raised a Fifth Amendment takings claim, and thus sought just compensation (legal relief), did qualify since they dealt with questions of fact (Stedfast 1999).

Similarly, the Court ruled that the court of appeals did not err in allowing the jury to consider the question of the reasonableness of the city's land use decision. The Court held that the instructions to the jury limited its decision to the actions taken by the city on the land use permit in this particular case and did not deal with the question of the legitimacy of regulatory takings as an instrument of government. One might object that the distinction that is theoretically so clear in law, is easily muddled by a jury not familiar with land use regulations. That is, the jury is less likely to apply uniform standards in a consistent fashion than are judges versed in the law (Harvard 1999). It appears that the Court decision substitutes the jury for the judiciary in deciding if takings action is reasonable. As such, critics of the decision have noted that the Court has once again chosen to delegate decision making someone else.

In addition, one can argue that the basis of the jury decision on the criteria outlined in *Agins* confuses substantive due process functions with takings law (Higley 2000). While the former is meant to invalidate improper government action, the latter should be used to compensate property owners who suffer a property loss in the course of constitutionally acceptable regulation. It appears that no one, not the jury, certainly not the courts, recognized this distinction in *Del Monte Dunes*. If the city action was "irrational and unacceptable" as the jury decided, then it should have been invalidated by the jury, not subjected to monetary damages (Higley 2000).

Still, uniform standards did come out of *Del Monte Dunes*. The ripeness criteria and procedural requirements mentioned early in the case appear to have worked to clarify these two requirements. The district court had initially dismissed the landowner's claims as unripe, interpreting the city's actions as not final. This interpretation was reversed by the court of appeals, which found the city's action of rejecting five land use proposals over the course of five years as "sufficiently final" (Stedfast 1999). As such, the court appears to have once again established that protracted rejection can be interpreted as a final decision. The court also cited the lack of compensation procedures in place in California at the time of the final denial, as grounds for hearing the case. This seems to indicate that if states do not put such procedures in place, they can expect continued federal review of their land use decisions.

That state level land use policy will continue to be subject to federal court review seems to be a given, no matter what procedures for appeal are in place. *Palazzolo v. Rhode Island* {533 U.S. 606 (2001)} revisited the ripeness question, as well as whether pre-existing land use restrictions could be subject to a takings claim when the title of land is transfered. *Palazzolo* also considered the "geographic" basis of a taking claim, that is, how to define the boundaries of the parcel that is to serve as the basis of a claim of economic loss. Shying away from enunciating a categorical rule, the Court held that a state cannot "bar an individual who acquires property encumbered by a preexisting land use regulation from bringing an inverse condemnation action to challenge the regulation" (Harvard 2001). Preferring to decide each case on an ad hoc basis, the Court did leave open the possibility that the timing of acquisition could matter in such cases.

The case involved a parcel of wetlands on the Rhode Island coast, originally purchased by Palazzolo and his associates in 1959. After several unsuccessful attempts to develop the property in the 1960s, and following the loss of the corporate charter in 1978, the land passed automatically to Palazzolo, the corporation's lone remaining shareholder. By that time land use restrictions were in place and Palazzolo's two subsequent requests to develop the wetlands portion of the property were deemed not to meet the "compelling public purpose" criteria in place. Palazzolo lost his administrative appeal of the council actions and proceeded to file an inverse condemnation action in state court, arguing the council actions constituted a "total taking" that deprived his property of "all economically beneficial use" (Harvard 2001). After denial at the trial court level, Palazzolo appealed to the Supreme Court of Rhode Island. That court found that the claim should be denied on ripeness grounds. It also added that his case failed on the merits since there was still a portion of his property that could be developed, and as such the wetlands regulations had not deprived him of all "economically beneficial use" of his property (Harvard 2001). The Rhode Island high court also noted that a key component of the *Penn Central* test was a property owner's "reasonable investment-backed expectations." Given the timing of the property transfer, after the wetlands regulations were in effect, the court held that Palazzolo could not reasonably have expected to develop the portion of the parcel effected by the regulations.

The Supreme Court found that Palazzolo's claim was ripe, that the automatic bar to challenging pre-existing regulation was unreasonable, and that the state high court was correct in rejecting the total takings claim. In deciding the ripeness question, Justice Kennedy, writing for the five person majority, argued that when "the permissible uses of property are *known to a reasonable degree of certainty*" a claim is ripe (Kmiec 2001).

The case was remanded to state court to be decided as a partial taking, using the *Penn Central* criteria to render a judgement. The justices actually split on the question of the timing of the purchase and its effect on expectations. Justice O'Connor, who was in the majority, expressed the sentiment that some consideration should be given to existing regulations in deciding what constitutes reasonable economic expectations. A view that was repeated by Ginsberg in the minority dissent and joined by three other justices, and in turn attacked by Scalia in his concurrence with the majority. The suggestion that timing matters is bound to confuse the lower courts, since it was not an actual part of the majority opinion, but clearly represents a view of a majority bloc.

The current case before the Court, *Tahoe-Sierra Preservation Council v. Tahoe Regional Planning Agency (TRPA)* (121 S. Ct. 2589, 2001) addresses the question of a temporary moratorium on land development, and if such action constitutes a taking. At issue is the land use plan developed by the Tahoe Regional Planning Agency and the thirty-two month development moratorium in place between 1981-1984. Although little in the way of development has occurred in the Tahoe region for the past two decades, the suit only considers the original 32-month period. The federal appeals court for San Francisco ruled that "temporary development moratoria promote effective planning" and should not be considered a taking(Greenhouse 2002). While the appeals court followed the reasoning in *First English*, one of the dissenting judges pointed out that they were following the dissent, not the majority opinion in the case (Kanner 2001).

In oral arguments before the Supreme Court, the attorney for the 442 property owners party to the suit argued that "[w]henever there is a flat-out prohibition on using your land, whether it's for a day or a decade, it's a taking" (Savage 2002). This extreme position appears to trouble some of the previously pro-property rights justices, with Justice Kennedy mentioning the World Trade Center site in a hypothetical, and Justice Stevens suggesting the counsel was claiming a distinction that was not all that clear in reality. While the Court has taken a decidedly pro-property stance in recent rulings, the fact that the solicitor general, Theodore B Olson, has sided with the agency, may give the Justices pause to rethink their normally conservative tendencies.

The Court as an Agenda Setter

The legal history of the regulatory taking issue has shown that the Supreme Court has yet to provide a definitive answer as to what governmental actions constitute a taking. True, there are rough outlines that provide some guidance, but the Court simply refuses to issue categorical criteria. No doubt this reluctance can be explained in part by the series of 5-4 decisions that characterize recent cases. While one can identify a property rights bloc—Scalia, Rhenquist, Kennedy, O'Connor, and Thomas—it is harder to identify a lasting, clearly enunciated, property rights rationale that ties the voting bloc together. Rather, when deciding on takings, the Court prefers an ad hoc, case-by-case mode of action.

To date, except in the very narrow case when a government regulation deprives an owner of all "economically viable" use of the land, the Court has refused to issue categorical standards to be used to determine when regulation constitutes a taking. Instead, the Court has based its rulings on a reasoning that appears to be continually evolving, with only the broadest and vaguest outlines, such as the "too far" edict, the "bundle of property rights" theory, and the "essential nexus" condition, offered as parts of an indefinite formula. While recent rulings have favored the property owner, and have been viewed as victories by the property rights movement, the lack of clear precedents and the cost of bringing suit make the judicial system something short of the ideal refuge for property owners seeking protection from governmental regulations.

Indeed, in the minds of some members of the property rights movement the legal history of this issue raises the question whether the courts are the appropriate venue to resolve the regulatory takings issue. Nancie Marzulla, of Defenders of Property Rights, suggests that they are not. In testimony before the House Committee on Resources in 1999, she asserted that it is the function of the legislative, not judicial, branch to balance competing social and economic concerns and arrive at a definition of a taking which need not be recreated on an ad-hoc basis each time the court is presented with the issue (Marzulla 1999). To bolster her claim she cited the former Chief Judge of the Court of Federal Claims, Loren Smith, who argued that courts "cannot produce comprehensive solutions. ... Judicial decisions are far less sensitive to societal problems than the law and policy made by the political branches of our great constitutional system" (Marzulla 1999). Clearly Marzulla, in expressing her frustration with the courts, was attempting to shift the debate over a definition of what constituted a takings back to a congressional venue. A subject we address in the next chapter.

CHAPTER FIVE

The Property Issue in Congress

For the most part, Congress is the ultimate destination of those who seek to control the agenda. The central role of Congress no doubt reflects its legislative role, as well as its institutional role as the bedrock of subsystem arrangements. That is, those who seek to alter the rules of the game or the course of public policy must go through Congress if they hope to make the deal stick. We are not arguing that agenda setting does not occur in other venues, nor are we suggesting that only legislation can be used to alter public policy. To do so would be naïve. Indeed, a myriad of studies have demonstrated how bureaucracy, the courts, interest groups, the executive, etc., alter the implementation of public policy with no actual change in law. Rather, we suggest that Congress, as the primary legislative body in the polity, not to mention its role as the institutional bedrock of policy subsystems, is usually the first stop for those who seek to change public policy.

The third chapter tracked the origins and evolution of the modern environmental movement, suggesting that it became institutionalized in Congress by the mid-1970s. What that account underplayed was the role of a rival subsystem, dealing with public lands, that predates the establishment of the environmental subsystem. The public lands subsystem is arguably among the first such relationships developed by Congress. Like its environmental counterpart, it was institutionalized in a committee system that granted jurisdiction over public lands issues to select standing committees in the late nineteenth century.

Over time the bulk of pubic lands issues were consolidated into the jurisdiction of a single committee in both chambers, aptly named Pubic Lands (the predecessor of the current Resources and Natural Resources committees). For the first half of the twentieth century the Public Lands committees served as the gatekeepers for the myriad issues dealing with public lands—everything from grazing permits to mining went through the committees. The committees, most members of Congress, and the public tended to view, and understand, public lands issues in economic terms. That is, the natural resources of the nation were defined as economic resources, ripe for the taking. The only question to be settled involved who was to do the taking, and under what conditions. In this sense, while natural resources and public lands were defined as so many economic opportunities, there was always some consideration of conservation and sustainability.

The story told in the third chapter highlights how these subtexts become the dominant refrain in the 1970s. That said, the environmental subsystem coexists with a public lands subsystem that tends to promote multiple use of the nation's natural resources. This chapter focuses on how the emphasis on economic use is altered as a result of the environmental movement, which itself becomes the focus of a counter-mobilization on the part of property rights advocates.

The congressional agenda setting drama consists of several acts, legislative introduction and referral, committee hearings, the dance of legislation as it occurs on the floor, all of which are repeated in the other chamber. Since little in the way of takings legislation has made it to the floor of either chamber, we concentrate our attention in this chapter on the first and second acts in the drama. We begin with the initial stage of setting the congressional agenda, legislative introductions and referrals. The chapter then moves on to discuss the role of committee hearings in controlling the property rights agenda. It closes with a discussion of recent legislative efforts, highlighting the role of policy entrepreneurs and the change in party control of Congress on the efforts to set the property rights agenda.

Setting the Congressional Agenda: Legislative Introductions

Agenda control is a central preoccupation of Congress. While most studies cut to the chase and focus on the role of committees as guardians, entrepreneurs, or obstacles in setting the agenda, we begin with a look at what is arguably the initial, and too often overlooked, first step in the process—legislative introductions and referrals. The introduction of legislation is important because it serves as an indicator of congressional interest in an issue or policy area. While the introduction of legislation would appear to cost a member of Congress little in the way of time and resources, sponsorship of legislation is not simply an exercise in symbolic politics. Members are careful to think through the consequences of introducing legislation or cosponsoring a bill, considering both how the legislation changes the status-quo and the potential effect on important segments of their constituency.

On the flip side, an increase in legislative introductions in a particular policy area is carefully monitored by the effected committee(s). Any increase indicates that an issue has heated up, and may represent a challenge to the policy status-quo. Committees jealously guard their role as gatekeeper, taking care that legislation dealing with matters under their jurisdiction is referred to them exclusively. Indeed, competition over legislative referrals tell one a good deal about who controls the congressional agenda. The neglect of legislative referrals by those interested in agenda setting is odd, given that Woodrow Wilson (1885, 1973, 63) noted "[t]he fate of bills committed [to committee] is generally not uncertain. As a rule, a bill committed is a bill doomed." Quite simply, Wilson recognized legislative referral as an important means of controlling the congressional agenda. Recent scholarship has reinforced this observation, suggesting that turf wars are fought to control agenda access (King 1994, 1997; Worsham 1998). Committees act as gatekeepers vis-à-vis their control of legislative referrals in policy areas of interest to themselves and their allies. While bill introduction serves as both a signal of congressional interest in a topic, and may also serve as an attempt to alter the status quo, nothing comes of legislation unless a committee decides to act.[1]

Property Issue in Congress

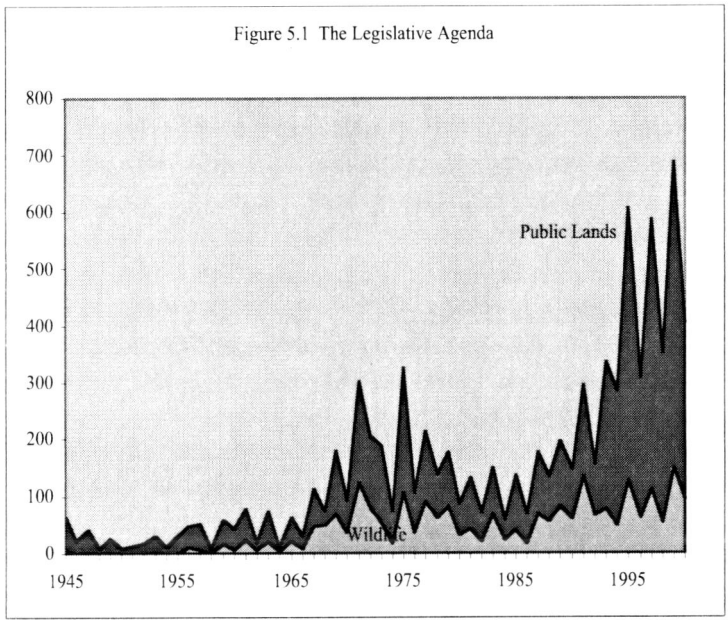

Figure 5.1. Annual number of public lands and wildlife bills introduced in Congress.

As discussed in chapter three, the takings movement is a disparate collection of interests who came together to decry the effects of public policy intended to regulate the use of public and private resources. The origins of the movement in the sagebrush rebellion and wise-use movement, both of which were primarily focused on regulation governing the use of public lands, informed the construction of our search for relevant legislation. Using the *Congressional Record* and *Thomas* (a web-based resource maintained by the Library of Congress) we searched for any legislation dealing with public land use and regulation between 1945 and 2000. [2] All told this involved gathering information on 8331 pieces of legislation (1620 wildlife bills and 3672 public land bills in the House, 844 wildlife bills and 2195 public land bills in the Senate). The results of the search are reproduced in figure 5.1, which tracks the salience of public lands issues on the congressional agenda between 1945 and 1998.

Figure 5.1 tracks two types of legislation, that dealing with public land use and legislation focusing on wildlife habitat protection.[3] Arguably, these two types of legislation represent the dominant coalitions—economic and conservationist—active in the policy realm. Review of figure 5.1 reveals that the use of public resources was not really contested until the late 1960s, when wildlife conservation legislation worked its way onto the agenda. After the "big-bang" associated with the modern environmental movement in 1968, wildlife legislation comes to represent a significant portion of the legislation introduced. Even then, its near parity with public land legislation is episodic at best. Indeed, every period in which there is a surge in wildlife bills also produces a similar leap in public lands bill. By 1990 public lands legislation dwarfs conservation legislation, suggesting bills considering the economic use of public resources dominate the debate.

The action-reaction phenomenon appears to fit the mobilization-counter mobilization scenario discussed in chapter two. The initial surge of wildlife bills associated with the growth in conservation and environmental protection activity on the part of the federal government is met by a similar increase in economic use legislation. The reaction carries over into the latter part of the decade and coincides with President Jimmy Carter's efforts to rewrite Western land use and water policy, actions that generated a significant congressional response. The second big push includes the post-Reagan era and reflects in part a reaction to the increased activity of the property rights "movement" discussed in the previous chapter.

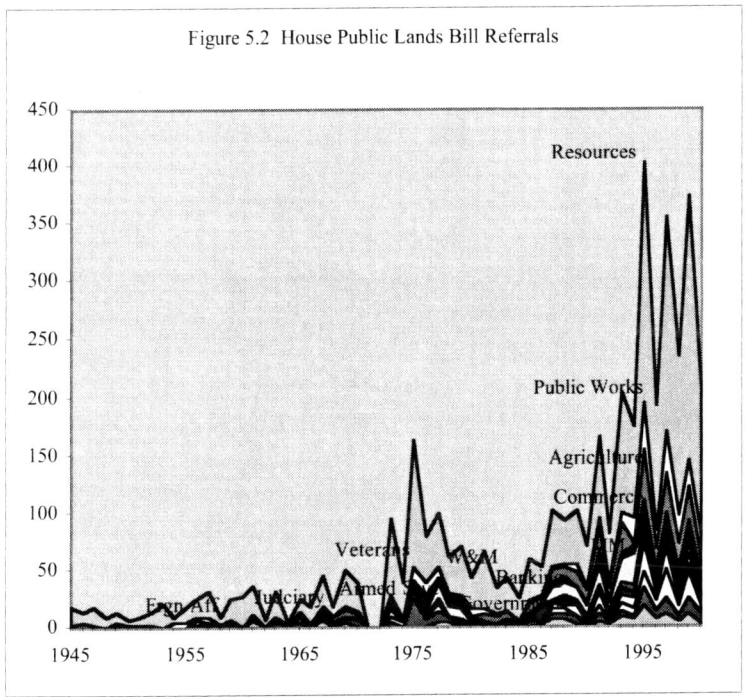

Figure 5.2. The referral of House public lands bills to committee. Trend lines are the number of bills referred to particular committees, by year.

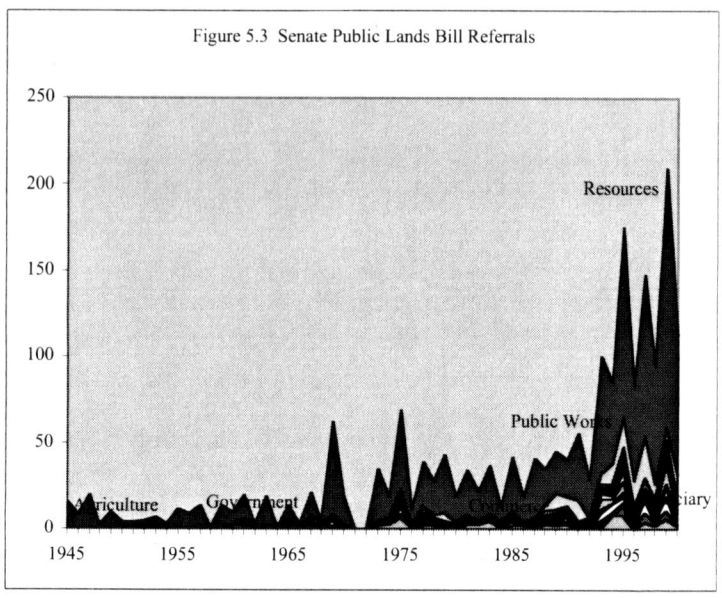

Figure 5.3. The referral of Senate public lands bills to committee. Trend lines are the number of bills referred to particular committees, by year.

Since bill introduction is often an attempt to alter the status quo, it is not a stretch to conclude that the management of public lands is contested during these periods of increased activity. Quite simply, the 1970s and mid-1990s were periods of intense agenda setting activity, a time when the management of public lands was high on the congressional agenda.

To say that the issue was on the agenda, and that its salience increased over time, tells us little about how it was processed by Congress, a topic to which we now turn.

Figures 5.2, 5.3, 5.4, and 5.5 map legislative referrals in public lands and wildlife issues in the House and Senate between 1945 and 2000. The trend lines represent the number of bills referred to distinct committees over the period 1945-2000 and were gathered from the *Congressional Record*.

Figures 5.2 and 5.3 document the domination of the public land agenda in the House and Senate, respectively, by the Resources committee since 1945.[4] The competition that does occur in the referral game coincides with the increase in the number of bills introduced. That said, the bulk of legislation remains in the realm of the Resources Committees even during these periods of increased salience. When contrasting the House and Senate, one notices that competition in any form is rare in the latter. This is probably the result of the ability of Senators to add non-germane amendments to legislation reported out of committee, making competition via legislative referrals only one means of shaping the legislative agenda in the Senate.

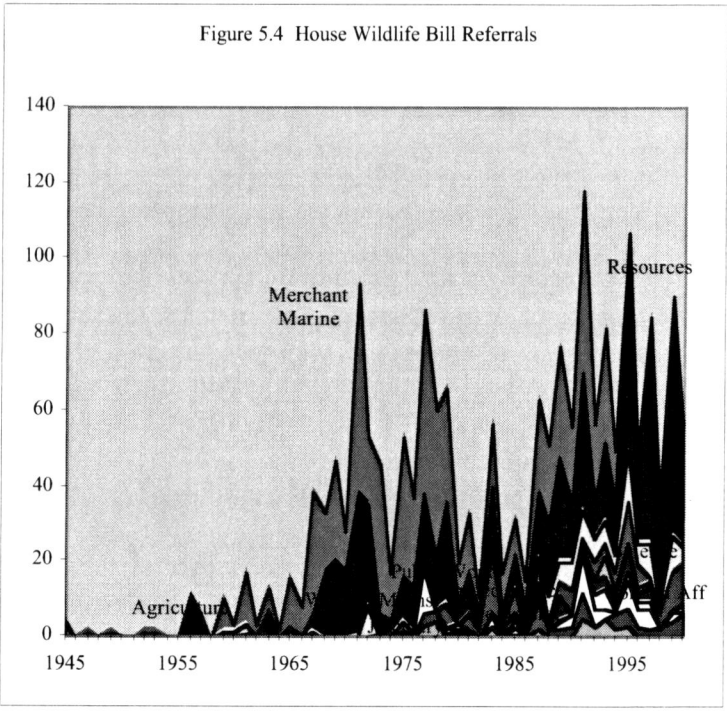

Figure 5.4. The referral of House wildlife bills to committee. Trend lines are the number of bills referred to particular committees, by year.

Compare the situation in public lands legislation with that of wildlife legislation. As was the case in public lands, increased legislative activity is associated with increased competition in referrals. This time the competition is more intense, with the Resources Committee and the Merchant Marine and Fisheries

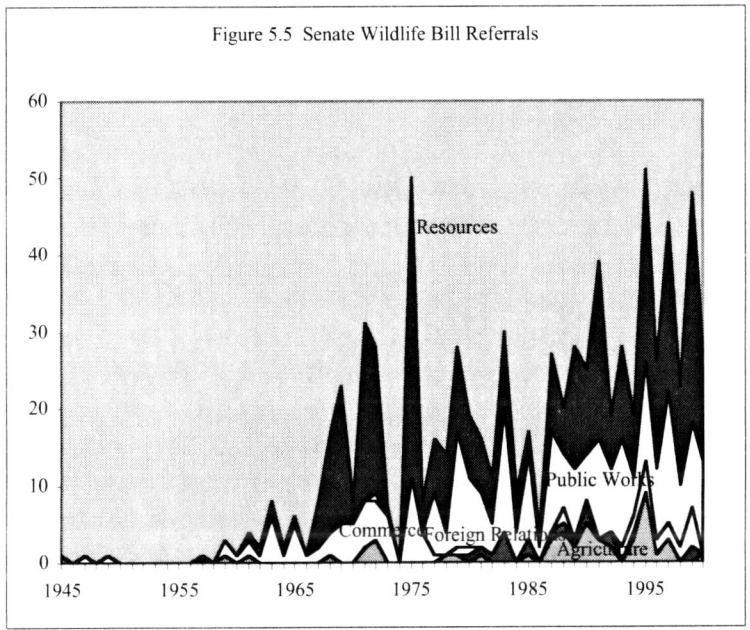

Figure 5.5 The referral of Senate wildlife bills to committee. Trend lines are the number of bills referred to particular committees, by year.

Committee neck and neck in the House until the latter's policy responsibilities are reassigned to the former in the late 1990s (figure 5.4). Similarly, the Senate Environment and Public Works Committee is locked in a seemingly permanent struggle for control of the wildlife agenda with the Energy and Natural Resources Committee from the mid 1970s onward (figure 5.5). The more competitive nature of bill referrals in the wildlife subsystem is a reflection of both its recent vintage, it does not really take off until the rebirth of environmentalism in the 1960s, and its nature—regulatory policy as opposed to the distributive cast of most public lands policy. No doubt the competition reflects the jockeying for position and control that accompanies the establishment of any policy realm. It also is a byproduct of policy that seeks to regulate, or even redistribute, the costs of "doing business" on public lands.

In summary, public lands legislation has been a permanent feature on the congressional agenda since the Second World War. During the first decade and half of that period public lands policy was primarily distributive in nature. A survey of bill titles reveal that the bulk of legislation is concerned with economic exploitation—primarily extending mineral and grazing leases to private parties. In the early 1960s this changes with the introduction of wildlife preservation as a concern. By the late 1960s conservation concerns were a permanent topic in the discussion of public lands use. While the bulk of public lands bills treat the issue as a distributive matter—who gets mineral, grazing, and water rights, and under what conditions—wildlife legislation offered a new definition of natural resources. Clearly, the rise in the number of wildlife bills was an attempt to redefine the issue. An attempt that enjoyed limited success given the role of the Resource committees as the institutional bedrock of the public lands policy subsystem in both chambers. Our examination of legislative referrals demonstrates that the Resource committees are the ultimate destination of most public lands legislation, even during the periods of turf wars that flare up from the late 1960s onward. Indeed, the Resource committees are the initial destination of the first wildlife bills in the 1950s, although by the late 1960s rival committees have established a claim to wildlife turf in both the House and Senate. Still, rather than dominating wildlife turf, these committees are forced to accommodate the Resource committees as co-partners in the policy realm.

Committees as Gatekeepers: Hearings and Turf Control

Ever since Woodrow Wilson (1885; 1973, 69) suggested that "Congress in its committee-rooms is Congress at work," the congressional committee system has been the center of congressional scholars attention (Fenno 1966, 1973; Shepsle 1978, 1979; Krehbiel, Shepsle, and Weingast 1987; Smith and Deering 1990; Krehbiel 1991; Hall 1993; Brown 1995; Worsham 1998). The conventional view of committee jurisdictions is that they are stable with distinct areas of specialization. This arrangement allows committees to claim jurisdiction over particular issue areas. Bills are referred to substantive committees according to their established jurisdictions, and committees are prohibited from initiating legislative hearings where they lack jurisdiction (Fenno 1966, 1973; Froman 1967). Some have suggested that this jurisdictional arrangement, in which committees treat turf as if it conveyed exclusive property rights, obstructs significant change by conceding agenda control to those with an established interest in the continuation of the status-quo (see King 1997).

Contemporary research into committee jurisdictions has revealed a more dynamic environment than that proposed by earlier studies. Studies of the post-reform era Congress report the infrequency of jurisdictional monopolies and the increasing tendency for jurisdictions to overlap (Jones and Strahan 1985; King 1992; Young and Cooper 1993; Jones, Baumgartner, and Talbert 1993; King 1997; Worsham 1998). While these studies reinforce previous findings regarding the significant influence of committees over the content of legislation referred to them, they also document how different committee venues favor different interests. Thus, jurisdictional control is pivotal to the legislative process, agenda setting, and the shape of public policy.

Setting the decision agenda: The strategic use of hearings

Congressional hearings serve multiple purposes. They may be an initial foray into a policy area, used primarily to gather information to aid in understanding the causes or interpreting the meaning of an event. In this regard they are often a preliminary first step in deciding whether an item should be moved to the government agenda. These hearings are quite often non-legislative, in that no particular piece of legislation is the subject of the hearing. Recent studies of committee jurisdiction have focused on the role of non-legislative hearings as a means of establishing claims to both new and established policy turf (King 1994, 1997; Talbert, Jones, and Baumgartner 1995; Worsham 2000). Since there are few restrictions on the topics that any subcommittee may investigate, non-legislative hearings enable committee leaders to expand their jurisdictional boundaries into policy areas not normally considered their turf. By holding investigative hearings on a particular issue a committee can make a claim to expertise in the area, increasing the odds that future legislation will be referred to the committee. This process can lead to the disruption of jurisdictional monopolies and a change in established policy.

As the gatekeepers to a particular policy realm, committees quite often hold hearings to consider changes in public policy. In this fashion hearings serve as a means of promoting or "boosting" an issue by framing it as a public problem, often with a solution (in the form of a bill) attached. As such, legislative hearings are an indicator that an issue has made its way to the decision agenda. Committees jealously guard their turf and use both established rules, such as Rule X in the House, and precedent to ensure the parliamentarian refers legislation dealing with matters under their jurisdiction to them.

Hearings are also a means of overseeing the implementation of existing policy. In this oversight mode they may be judgmental or "critical" of the way in which public policy is carried out or the effects it produces. As such, hearings serve as a means of instructing bureaucrats in the proper implementation of the program in question (Griffith 1951). In the oversight mode hearings may also serve as a means of advocating policy alternatives previously dismissed, especially when rival interests are invited to testify (Hinckley 1971; Aberbach 1990). One point is certain. Hearings are held with strategic intent, as evident by the topics chosen for investigation and the type of witnesses invited to testify (Talbert, Jones, and Baumgartner 1995).

We opened our study by suggesting that recent studies of agenda setting are concerned with how the definitions of policy issues change over time (Baumgartner and Jones 1991, 1993). Change in issue definition is often a product of change in committee jurisdiction in Congress. That is, new definitions of a problem, and the solution(s) to it, are closely correlated with changes in committee jurisdiction. This phenomenon was evidenced in Christopher Bosso's (1987) study of the pesticide issue. As long as pesticides were considered as tools of farmers, the Agricultural Committees in the House and Senate enjoyed exclusive jurisdiction over pesticide use and regulation. As attention shifted toward the environmental aspects of pesticides use, jurisdiction was contested. In the end, multiple committees claimed a stake in the matter of pesticides use, leading to the adoption of more restrictive regulation. Thus, the interaction of issue definition and jurisdictional change may often facilitate changes in policy outcomes (Talbert, Jones, and Baumgartner 1995).

We begin our analysis of hearing activity with an overview of the jurisdictional dynamics of public land policy since the Second World War, highlighting how conservation concerns came onto the scene and altered the debate in the 1970s. We then move on to document the entry of "property rights" into the debate, finding support for our contention that it was a reaction to the inroads of the conservation and environmental movements in the shaping of public land policy.

Controlling the Public Lands Agenda

Figures 5.6 and 5.7 track hearing activity in the public lands policy realm between 1946 and 1998 in the House and Senate, respectively. The bulk of the data, covering the years 1946-1994, come from the data set compiled by Frank R. Baumgartner and Bryan D. Jones as part of their ongoing Agendas Project.[5]

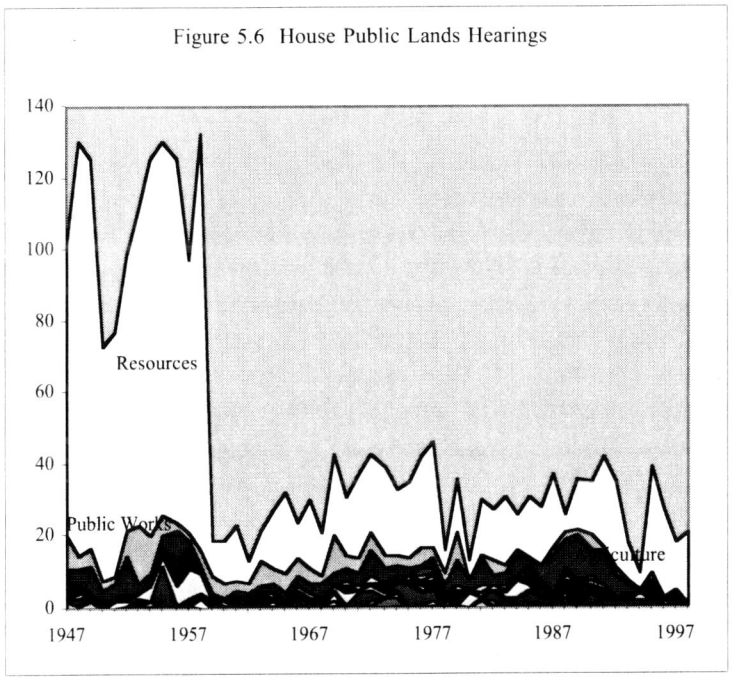

Figure 5.6. The annual number of House public lands hearings, by committee. Source for 1946-1994, Baumgartner and Jones, Agendas Project Data Set.

The data for 1995-1998 was collected using the Congressional Information Service (CIS) Index to Committee Hearing and Hearings Abstracts, using the keyword "public lands," to locate all hearings dealing with public lands issues. The figures enable one to track both the level of hearing activity, as well as to determine the identity of the committees holding hearings. Unlike the legislative referral portion of the chapter we do not distinguish wildlife from public lands hearings, combining the two for ease of presentation.

A review of the figures reveals that the House is subject to a good deal more hearing competition than is the Senate. While the Resources/Natural Resources Committees are clearly involved in efforts to control the public lands agenda in each chamber, after 1958 competition increases in the House and the number of hearings actually drops. The major House competitors to the Resources hearing monopoly are the Agriculture and Public Works Committees, although a variety of committees are involved periodically. That said, any increase in hearing activity by a committee other than Resources is matched by a similar increase in activity by the Resources Committee. This suggests that while there is some competition, Resources manages to maintain its place as the bedrock of public lands policy. Compare the situation in the House to that of the Senate (figure 5.7).

Property Issue in Congress   91

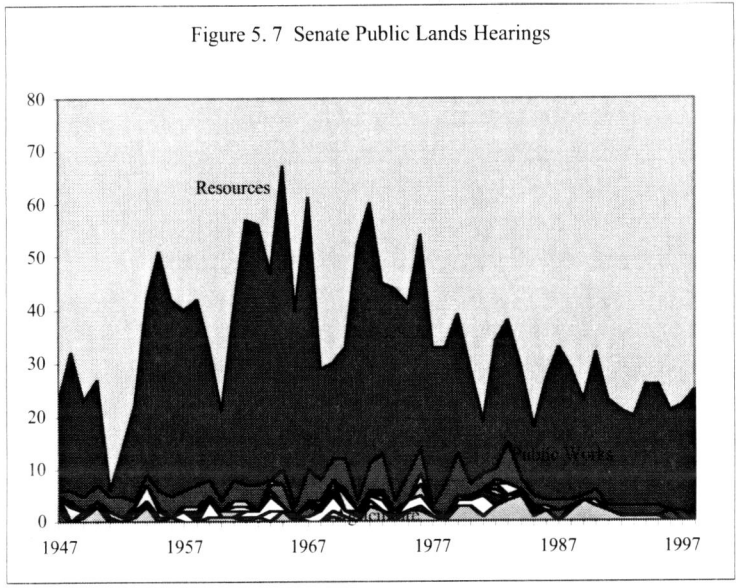

Figure 5.7. The annual number of Senate public lands hearings, by committee. Source for 1946-1994, Baumgartner and Jones, Agenda Project Data Set.

While the Resources Committee does not enjoy a perfect monopoly in the Senate, it does appear to enjoy the lion's share of the hearing market in the Senate, qualifying it for near monopoly status. Indeed, only Public Works has any kind of sustained hearing presence in the Senate. The hearing situation in both chambers mirrors the dynamic involved in the referral of legislation, suggesting control over legislative referrals is a good indicator of control over the policy realm.

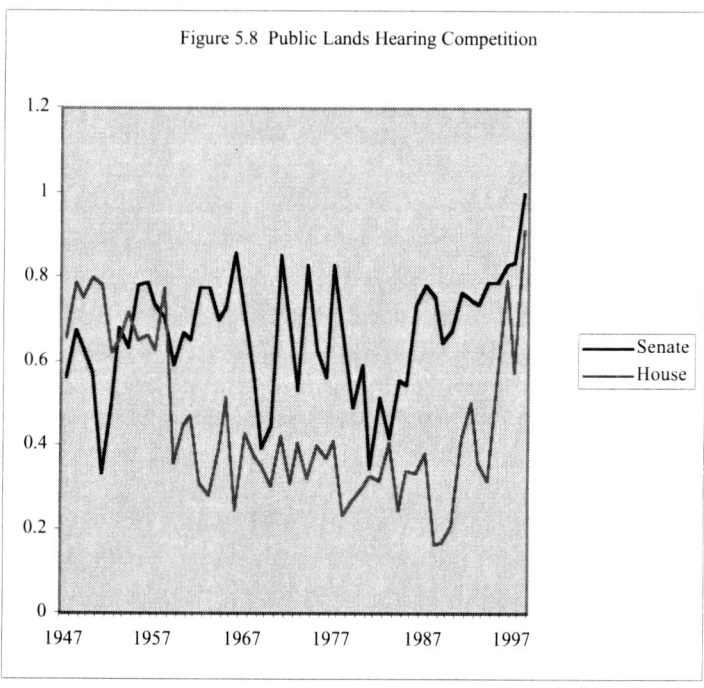

Figure 5.8. Herfindahl index of hearing competition in public lands, by year. A score close to 1 indicates a near monopoly on hearings.

In order to get a better feel for the level of jurisdictional competition, we constructed Herfindahl Index scores for each chamber. Squaring the proportion of committees holding hearings in the policy realm and then summing the squares of those proportions, results in a Herfindahl index score. The result is an indicator of turf control in which a score of 1 indicates a single committee holds all hearings and a score close to zero means hearings are spread out evenly among a large number of committees.[6] Tracking the Herfindhal index score (figure

5.8) for the Senate demonstrates how tightly the Natural Resources Committee controls the public lands policy realm in that chamber. Compare the Senate monopoly to the House situation, where after 1958 competition picks up with the Resources, Public Works, and Agriculture committees all vying for a piece of the hearing action. Indeed, it is not until 1995 that the House index score climbs above .5 and approaches the level of monopoly sustained in the Senate. Clearly, hearing competition is higher in the House, where a wider variety of committees provide a sustained challenge to the Committee on Natural Resources efforts to control the agenda.

So, what does competition produce in the way of policy outcomes? The assumption is that different hearing venues provide opportunities for new ideas to enter the policy stream and rival interests to get in on a piece of the action. In an effort to determine if either occurred we utilized the Congressional Information Service (CIS) Index to Committee Hearing and Hearings Abstracts, to identify congressional hearings that dealt specifically with property rights issues. This offers a more limited number of hearings than contained in the public lands search. We included only those hearings found under the key words: eminent domain, land use, property, right of property, right-of-way and easements; and those under the subcategories private property or right of property under the term environmental protection.

The search allows us to track when the property rights issue is raised in the public lands domain, identify the committees that consider it, and calculate the mix of private interests involved at hearings concerned with property rights questions. In most cases the search simply involved noting the group affiliation of witnesses as listed in the Hearing Abstracts portion of the CIS. In some instances we read the abstracted version of testimony to determine affiliation.

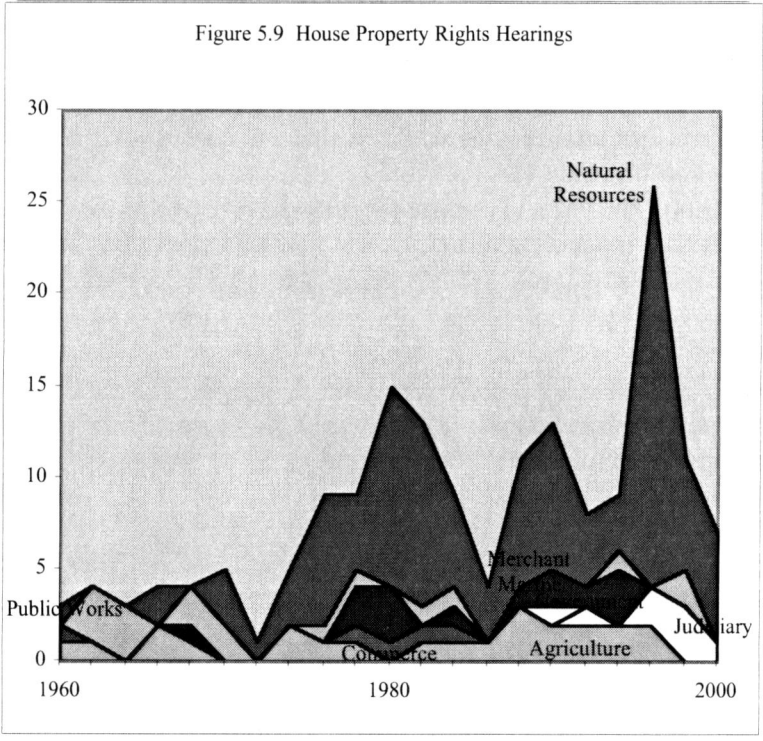

Figure 5.9. The annual number of House property hearings, by committee.

We are primarily interested in distinguishing among environmental protection, conservation, economic, and property rights interests. We stuck to a fairly conservative coding scheme, only including an actor in one of the categories if it was clear from their group affiliation or statements in the Abstracts the interest with which they were affiliated. Once again, we are simply trying to get a feel for how the universe of private interests changes as the hearing venue changes or with the passage of time. All told, 301 hearings were reviewed, 171 in the House and 130 in the Senate, between 1959 and 2000.

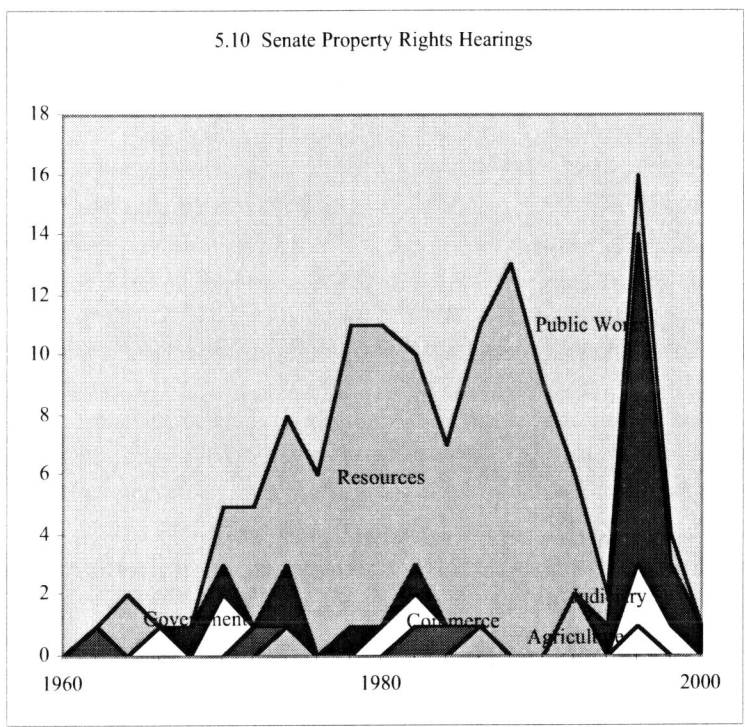

Figure 5.10. The annual number of Senate property hearings, by committee.

Figures 5.9 and 5.10 track hearing activity dealing with property rights in the House and Senate, respectively. In light of the smaller volume of activity, hearings are aggregated into two-year congressional sessions for ease of presentation. A quick perusal of figure 5.9 reveals that competition is not as intense in the House as it was in the public lands case. That said, the major committee players in public lands are also active when the issue of property rights comes up—the Agriculture, Public Works, and Natural Resources committees are all a constant presence, with the latter more clearly in control when the topic of property rights is raised. In addition, Merchant Marine and Fisheries is a fairly regular presence during the period under study, reinforcing the findings in the section on legislative referrals. At first glance, committee competition appears to be even rarer in the Senate (see figure 5.10). The Natural Resources Committee is the dominant venue through 1994, with only a brief interlude of competition in 1970. All that changes in 1996 when the Environment and Public Works Committee come onto the scene and dominates the hearing market through 2000. Comparison of the Herfindahl index scores for the property rights hearings with those for public lands, supports the impression that as questions of property rights are raised, committee competition decreases.[7]

In order to determine if the change in venue effects the interpretation of the problem, we calculated the fraction of economic versus environmental interests invited to testify at hearings in each venue. Our reasoning is that hearing dominated by one or the other will tend to favor that actor's interpretation of the issue. Perusing table 5.1 allows one to distinguish committees that appear to favor one interest over the other. In the House, the Judiciary, Commerce, and Public Works committees have an obvious soft spot for economic interests. Similarly, the Agriculture and Natural Resources committees tend to favor economic interests over environmental actors, although not with the supermajorities present in the previous three committees. Indeed, it is only in Merchant Marine and Fisheries that the environmental voice is in the majority. In the Senate, environmental interests garner a slight majority in the Resources Committee and they constitute a sizeable minority in both Agriculture and Public Works. Environmental interests are practically non-existent in hearings held by the Commerce, Government Operations and Judiciary Committees, all of which favor the economic interpretation of the question at hand.

What this suggests, not surprisingly, is that when questions of property arise, economic actors and their views are in the forefront. Still, the presence of environmental interests in many of the hearing venues means that with very few exceptions, economic views do not go unquestioned. Indeed, we are undoubtedly understating the influence of environmental views given that we leave out the vast bulk of hearings that deal exclusively with environmental policy. Remember, we only included environmental hearings dealing with property matters. That said, the public lands subsystem remains one dominated by economic interests, with some venues tone-deaf to the environmental tune—the Judiciary and Commerce Committees in particular. In the case of public lands policy there is not so much a counter-mobilization, as there is sustained (institutionalized) control.

Table 5.1 The Correspondence Between Committee Venue and Type of Witness

House Committee*	Type of Witness	
	Environment	Property
Agriculture	42	58
Commerce	29	71
Government Operations	50	50
Judiciary	0	100
Merchant Marine	63	37
Natural Resources	44	56
Public Works	28	72
Senate Committee**		
Agriculture	41	59
Commerce	13	87
Government Operations	17	83
Judiciary	03	97
Natural Resources	50	50
Public Works	43	57

NOTE: Figures are the percentage of witnesses
*Phi = .17; chi-square (6 df = 75.05) (p<.00001)
**Phi = .21; chi-square (5 df = 66.27) (p<.00001)

Property Rights Legislation

We began this chapter with a macro-level overview of the treatment of public lands and wildlife legislation. We chose this level of analysis based on the belief that a good deal of the ire of the property rights movement was directed at government efforts to curtail the use of public lands, or force private landowners to consider the effect their actions have on endangered species, water quality, and other public concerns. We then narrowed our focus to consider the role of hearings in maintaining turf control over public lands, suggesting that while property rights interests made inroads, they did not appear to gain control over more than a few committee venues. In this final section we move to a micro-level examination of the entrepreneurs involved in the attempt to move the property rights issue to the top of the agenda. We open with a discussion of the various types of property rights legislation, and then proceed to trace the efforts to set the congressional agenda over the last thirty years.

Essentially, any piece of legislation that intends to protect the property owner from having to carry a disproportionate burden of a government action may be viewed as a property rights bill. Since 1973, eighty-two property rights bills have been introduced in Congress (see Appendix 1 for complete listing of introduced property rights legislation from 1977 - 2001).[8] A close look at the content of the bills introduced in Congress indicates that property rights legislation usually serves any of five objectives. The five categories of property rights legislation are: symbolic (S); eminent domain assessment (EDA); eminent domain compensation (EDC); takings assessment (TA); and, takings compensation (TC). A brief description of each type of property rights legislation follows.

Symbolic legislation seeks to increase awareness of an issue often through some type of public ceremony.[9] Only one piece of symbolic legislation was introduced in Congress over the course of our study. House Joint Resolution 261, introduced by Gladys Noon Spellman (D-Md) was intended to designate the third week in April "National Private Property Week." The bill was referred to the Post Office and Civil Service Committee, where, as

Woodrow Wilson would have predicted, it was never heard from again.

Eminent domain assessment (EDA) legislation seeks to establish policies and procedures, including restriction and exchange requirements, to be followed by federal agencies prior to the acquisition of private lands or an interest in private lands. As such, EDA legislation often seeks to restrict the situations in which the government can exercise its power of eminent domain. Given the long history of the government using such power, EDA legislation is among the most common type of property rights legislation. An example of EDA legislation is HR 8141, the "Bill to amend the Uniform Relocation Assistance and Real Property Acquisition Policies Act of 1970," introduced in 1980 by Albert Ullman (D-Or). Among other things, HR 8141 would have required a federal agency to prepare a Land Acquisition Plan (LAP) before acquiring lands or an interest in lands. LAPs called on government agencies to balance the need for acquisition against the costs and impacts on private landowners and state and local governments. HR 8141 also established a Land Policy Group charged with developing uniform land acquisition procedures and reviewing the appeals by private land owners, or state and local governments, of federal land acquisitions.

Eminent domain compensation (EDC) legislation seeks to establish guidelines to be used in reimbursing real property owners for the costs incurred as a result of any federal project or act of condemnation by a federal agency. An example of such legislation is Senate bill 1108, the "Uniform Relocation Assistance Act Amendments of

1979." Introduced by James Sasser (R-Tn) S 1108 was an effort to amend the Uniform Relocation Assistance and Real Property Acquisition Policies Act of 1970 so as to require that relocation benefits, including relocation assistance advisory services, be made available to all persons displaced by the commencement of a federal or federally assisted project. The bill required the head of a federal agency administering or financing such a project to offer to acquire property from any person owning property affected by the project if they were left with an "uneconomic remnant" as a result of the exercise of eminent domain. Other examples of EDC legislation include bills offering compensation to ranchers and farmers for losses caused by the use of their lands, or adjacent lands, for missile ranges and military exercises.

Between 1977 and 1991, most of the property rights legislation introduced in Congress was the eminent domain compensation type (see Appendix 1). Beginning in 1991, property rights legislation that dealt more directly with the regulatory taking issue began appearing in Congress. Such legislation sought compensation for property owners whenever there was a diminution in the market value of their land caused by either a new law or regulation, or a governmental action under an existing law, such as the Endangered Species Act (Fellows 1996).

Like its eminent domain predecessors, taking legislation generally comes in two forms. The first, taking assessment (TA) legislation, is the logical offshoot of EDA legislation. These "look before you leap" statutes require government agencies to assess whether their actions might constitute a takings under either federal or state supreme court decisions (Cordes 1997). Taking assessment legislation is usually patterned after President Reagan's Executive Order 12630 and require some form of 'taking impact analysis' (TIA) before a federal agency could pursue any action which could result in a taking or diminution of the use or value of private property.[10] Typically, this also involves developing economic impact statements identifying and valuing the impacts of any proposed government regulation on private property. An example of a TA bill is HR 4418, or the "Private Property Rights Act of 1994," introduced by Pat Roberts (R-Ks). HR 4418 required federal agencies to certify to the Attorney General that a private property taking impact analysis had been completed before initiating any action that might result in a taking or diminution of use or value of private property. TA legislation is no doubt inspired by state level laws, often called Attorney General (AG) review bills, that require the state attorney general to develop guidelines to be used in determining whether state agency actions constitute a taking (Lund 1995).

The second type of takings legislation is referred to as takings compensation (TC) legislation. In most cases, the laws include the requirement for a takings impact analysis and establish a threshold at which a percentage diminution in value triggers the requirement for compensation, either for the lost value or for the entire value of the land. An example of a TC bill is HR 925, the "Private Property Protection Act of 1995," introduced by Charles Canady (R-Fl). HR 925 would have required compensation whenever regulatory diminished the fair market value of property by 20 percent or more. The bill also required the government to purchase at fair market value any portion of a property whose value has been diminished by more than 50 percent.

Exploring the rise in federal taking legislation

Since the inception of the Republic, the federal government has reserved the right to take private property when a public need requires it. Regulatory taking has its roots in this exercise of the power of eminent domain. It became a more common phenomenon following the passage of a spate of environmental and conservation legislation in the 1970s. Not surprisingly, opponents begin to explore the legislative approach to combating regulatory taking soon after. The legislation introduced in the 95th Congress (1977-1978) targeted the exercise of eminent domain and the treatment of real property in a 1970 act governing government reimbursement. While a continuation of the ongoing eminent domain dialogue, the legislation can be distinguished by its effort to carve out a new understanding of property rights for those whose property was subject to seizure. From reimbursing litigation expenses of property owners to granting them the right to choose to have the government move their real property to a suitable location, the bills sought to limit the manner in which the government treated a portion of condemned property. The legislation did not try to limit the power of eminent domain, or question its exercise by the government. Rather, it sought to protect property owners' interest in real property—houses, barns, and the like. As such, we suggest this legislation is a first, albeit minor, attempt to introduce the notion of "property rights" into the policy discussion.

The legislation introduced in the 96th Congress (1979-1980) continued the discussion of property rights. The Senate bill is a faithful replica of the preceding sessions House legislation, as are most of the House bills. New territory is staked out, however, by HR 6756, introduced by Lester Wolff (D-NY). The bill would have granted federal agencies the power to purchase "uneconomic remnants" of parts of property subject to eminent domain proceedings. As such, it recognized that the government using its powers of eminent domain on a portion of private property might make the remaining property worthless, or nearly so. Still, the bill left it up to the agency involved to determine if this was the case and whether or not to offer to purchase the remaining property.

The legislation introduced in the 97th Congress (1981-1982) continues the eminent domain compensation debate, with a new twist. HR 3691, introduced by Jamie Whitten (D-Ms), argues that those subject to eminent domain proceeding should have the right to jury trial in deciding on compensation. In moving the discussion of property rights to a question concerning the judicial venue, property rights advocates were able to move the congressional consideration of the issue to a different venue as well. Once the debate shifts to court room procedures, the Judiciary Committee claims a piece of the property rights turf. The jury trial argument is made again during the 98th Congress (1983-1984), with the result being the bulk of legislation is now referred to the Judiciary Committee. This trend continues through the 101st Congress (1989-1990), with legislation now focused on takings and the calculation of compensation when they occur.

This legislative route is subject to increased activity following the issuance of Executive Order 12630 by the Reagan administration in 1988. Executive Order 12630 required federal agencies to consider the taking implications of their regulations and to budget money to pay for necessary takings.[11] Most assessment type taking legislation is patterned after Executive Order 12630, and require some form of 'taking impact analysis' (TIA) before a federal agency could pursue any action which could result in a taking or diminution of the value of private property. Despite the objectives of Executive Order 12630, it suffered from two problems. First, it applied only to executive departments and agencies, and not to state and local government regulatory agencies. Second, and more importantly, the Clinton administration chose not to enforce the order (Lipford and Boudreaux 1995). As a result, proponents of taking legislation stepped up their efforts to enshrine the requirements of EO 12630 into law.

Four takings assessment bills (S 50 and HR 905, 1572 and 1650), intended to give Executive Order 12630 the force of law, were introduced in the 102nd Congress (1991-1992). All contained "private property rights" in their title, and sought to force government agencies to comply with EO 12630. The bills granted the Attorney General enforcement and oversight powers, compelling agencies to clear all activities that resulted in a taking with the Attorney General before acting. The legislation also tried to limit the power of judicial review to the procedural guidelines set out in the act, as opposed to questions regarding the right of the Attorney General to act as the taking traffic cop, or whether the activity in question did in fact constitute a taking. While none of the four were reported out of committee, they do mark an important turn in the property rights debate. In attempting to move the determination of an answer to the question of what constitutes a taking out of the courts and into the executive branch, they were a clear attempt to undercut both the judiciary, and for that matter Congress, by granting that authority to the president. In addition, the bills were cosponsored by sizeable fractions of each chamber. The Senate bill included 41 cosponsors and HR 1572 included 121 cosponsors. While these were overwhelmingly from the GOP, there were a handful of Democrats that signed on in each chamber, indicating the issue was becoming increasingly salient among the membership, or at least the GOP caucus.

1991 also saw the first taking compensation bill introduced in Congress. H.R. 2185, the "Just Compensation Act of 1991," introduced by R.F. Smith (R-Or), required the head of any federal agency acting under the authority of the Endangered Species Act, the Surface Mining Control and Reclamation Act, the National Trails System Act, or of the Federal Water Pollution Control Act, to compensate the owner of private property for any diminution in value caused by the action. H.R. 2185, like its taking assessment cousins, died in committee. That said, it is important for two reasons. First, it broadly labels enforcement activity associated with the preceding acts as "takings" and demands compensation for regulatory enforcement. Second, it too attracted a sizeable number of predominantly GOP cosponsors, 35 members signed on. Given Representative Smith's interest in agricultural matters, and the predominance of cosponsors from agriculture states, it is safe to suggest that the bill was primarily intended to aid farmers who were effected by wetlands regulation, species protection requirements, and the like.

The 103rd Congress (1993-1994) saw a continuation of the effort to bind federal agencies to EO 12630, with legislation introduced in both chambers (S 177, 2006, and HR 385, 561, 4418) mandating that all regulatory actions that might constitute a taking be cleared with the Attorney General before taking effect. The primary focus of at least some of the legislation still appeared to be regulation that effected agricultural interests. HR 561 was introduced by a Democrat from the California Central Valley, Gary Condit, and cosponsored by 112 members from primarily agriculture districts. The legislation introduced in the 103rd Congress contained a distinct partisan flavor, the GOP sponsored all but Condit's bill and even then constituted the bulk of the cosponsors of it. Indeed, protection of agricultural interests, while the favorite cover for those sponsoring takings legislation, was often only tangentially related to the bill in question. A perfect example was the "Farm, Ranch, and Homestead Protection Act of 1994," introduced by Kay Baily Hutchinson (R-Tx). The bill sought to prevent the Secretary of the Interior from adding additional species to the list of protected species or designating a species habitat as a critical habitat. It also excused federal agencies from the ESA requirement that they certify their actions did not endanger protected species or habitats, as well as providing compensation for individuals whose land suffered a loss in market value due to enforcement of the ESA.

Federal takings compensation legislation was again introduced in the 103rd Congress. H.R. 3875, introduced by Billy Tauzin (D-La)[12] and its Senate companion S. 1915, sponsored by Richard Shelby (R-Al), as well as HR 1388, sponsored by Robert Smith (R-Or), HR 3784 sponsored by Lamar Smith (R-Tx), and HR 3875, also sponsored by

Billy Tauzin (D-La), provided a right to compensation for property owners who suffered a diminution of property value. The target of the bills was more focused than the previous efforts, limiting their application to government action taken under the authority of the Endangered Species Act or under the section 404 wetlands program in the Federal Water Pollution Control Act. A related measure, S 2410, sponsored by Phil Gramm (R-Tx), extended the diminution of value concept to real property. The legislation established the "diminution of value" approach to compensation as the theme of choice of property rights advocates (Sax 1996). Perhaps more important, the legislation was proving an increasingly popular (HR 3875 had 165 cosponsors) and inter-chamber coordinated effort to get the takings issue on the congressional agenda. Still, no committee held a hearing to consider the legislation. Even the most popular bill, HR 3875, failed to garner a hearing, which led Representative Tauzin to file an unsuccessful "motion to discharge." The fate of the latter was no doubt sealed when the Judiciary Committee requested Executive Comment and the Department of Justice replied with an unfavorable assessment of the bill.

During the 104th Congress takings legislation gained new popularity in the House as part of the "Contract with America" (CWA), and for the first time gained access to the decision agenda when the GOP took control of the House following the 1994 elections. Attached to HR 9, the "Job Creation and Wage Enhancement Act of 1995," contained a provision that provided "compensation ... for any ... limitation or condition that is imposed by a final agency action on a use of property that would be lawful but for the agency action." The provision was to apply to any action that was "not negligible," defined as "any reduction in the value of property equal to 10 percent or more." The concept of "not negligible" was eventually altered and redefined as "any reduction of 20 percent or more," with an option for the property owner to require government purchase on any property subject to a reduction of 50 percent or more.

The compensation provision was seen as too severe to be taken seriously by any but true takings diehards (Sax 1996). Critics argued that a law requiring compensation for any agency action that results in a reduction of *any* lawful use of property was too absolute. For instance, such a law could require the public to pay pornographers, slum lords, and owners of leaking landfills to cease their activities, so long as no previous law prohibited that same conduct (Sax 1996).

Despite the criticism, HR 9 turned out to be the first instance of legislative success for the property rights proponents. The House passed the bill on March 3, 1995, also passing HR 925, the "Private Property Protection Act of 1995," which was incorporated into HR 9. HR 925, sponsored by Charles Canady (R-Fl), required the federal government to compensate property owners whenever regulatory action caused the value of any portion of their property to diminish by 20 percent or more. This latter legislation broadened the definition of what constituted a taking in that a government action need only affect a portion of the land in question, with the 20 percent test to be applied to that portion. H.R. 925, like its CWA counterpart, also provided the property owner the option of requiring the federal government to purchase any portion of land that was devalued by more than 50 percent as a result of an agency action. Even more ambitious than HR 3875, introduced in the previous Congress, HR 925 targeted not only actions falling under the Endangered Species Act and the wetlands provisions of the Water Pollution Control Act, it now included actions occurring under Federal Reclamation Law.[13]

The Senate companion bill (S 605) did not fare as well as its House counterpart. Introduced by the Republican Majority Leader, Robert Dole (R-Ks), the "Omnibus Property Rights Act of 1995" was reported out of the Senate Judiciary Committee but never made it to the floor, largely because its proponents lacked sufficient votes to break a threatened filibuster (McCutcheon et al. 1996). Opposition to the Senate bill focused on the lack of a coverage limitation (Sax 1996). Without a more narrowly focused definition of what constituted a taking, the Clinton administration and its Senate allies successfully argued that the conditions for compensation could be applied to just about any government action (Schmidt 1995). Another interesting feature of the Senate bill, and several of its Senate counterparts, was the reference to fifth-amendment guarantees of property rights. No doubt the reference was an attempt to build on the success of property rights claimants in recent court cases.

The 105th (1997-1998) Congress was a repeat of the 104th, with another legislative success for property rights proponents in the House that went nowhere in the Senate. HR 1534, the "Private Property Rights Implementation Act of 1997," introduced by Elton Gallegly (R-Ca) and cosponsored by 238 members, continued the fifth amendment line of argument initiated in the Senate. The bill authorized "an owner of private property to challenge the validity of any Federal agency action as a violation of the fifth amendment to the US Constitution in a district court or the United States Court of Federal Claims." In addition, the act required "a Federal agency that takes an agency action limiting the use of private property to give notice to the property owners explaining their rights and the procedure for obtaining any compensation that may be due to them." The bill passed the House 248-178, and was reported from the Senate Judiciary Committee, where it lingered on the legislative calendar until the session ended. Two other pieces of legislation (S 781 and 1204) quite similar to the House bill were subject to hearings in the Senate, although neither was reported from committee. A third bill (S 2271), also invoking the fifth amendment right to property, was placed directly on the legislative calendar, but failed to achieve cloture on a motion to proceed. Senator Orrin Hatch (R-Ut) acted as the point man for two of the Senate bills and the House measure, and while he proved able to work his will on the Judiciary Committee which he chaired, he proved less able to get his way on the Senate floor. While the property rights issue was attracting some Democrats, for the most part it was still viewed as a Republican cause.

The House, once again, took the lead in setting the property rights agenda during the 106th Congress (1999-2000) with two of the five pieces of legislation introduced reported from committee, and one passed in the chamber. Agency adherence to EO 12630 was once again a common theme on both chambers. HR 294, introduced by John Sweeney (R-NY), sought to bind agencies dealing with agricultural land to the Executive Order. S 246, sponsored by Chuck Hagel (R-Nb), sought adherence to EO 12630 in a round about fashion, relying on the OMB and the Attorney General to act as the clearing houses for agencies involved in a takings action. The Senate bill also exempted certain types of action, including the exercise of eminent domain, emergency actions, and military activity. Another theme from the past was revisited in HR 2550, introduced by Tom Delay (R-Tx), which sought to define diminution of value criteria to be applied when regulation limited what individuals could do with their property. HR 1142, sponsored by Don Young (R-Ak), sought to limit the enforcement of the ESA , requiring written permission from the owners of private property effected, a voluntary agreement, or a compensatory payment, before any effort at implementing the ESA took place. The bill was reported from committee, 27-11, but was never taken up on the House floor.

The legislation that made the greatest inroads in the 106th Congress dealt with access to the courts. HR 2372, introduced by Charles Canady (R-Fl) and cosponsored by 112 members, sought to expedite access to the Federal courts for those with takings claims and required agencies to notify individuals of their rights any time the agency engaged in a takings. The House bill was reported from the Judiciary Committee with a 14-7 vote and passed the House 226-182. While it resembled legislation introduced a month earlier in the Senate by Orrin Hatch (R-Ut), the bill was never acted on by the Senate Judiciary Committee.

The property rights debate continued through the first session of the 107th Congress, although it was muted compared to previous sessions. As of this writing, a single piece of legislation had been introduced in the Senate. S

1412, sponsored by Chuck Hagel (R-Nb), continued the effort to create a taking assessment requirement to govern all agency actions that might result in a taking of private property. There was slightly more legislative activity in the House, where John Sweeney (R-NY) kept his effort to resuscitate EO 12630 alive, once again with an agricultural focus. Representative Jo Ann Davis (R-Va) introduced legislation entitled "The Rural America Protection Act" (HR 2719), intended to force compensatory payment for lands designated wetlands. The final two pieces of legislation targeted the enforcement of the ESA, setting forth compensation guidelines for enforcement actions that diminished the value of private property (HR 472), or diminished the value of "any portion" of private property (HR 1403). To date, none of this legislation has been subject to hearing.

The Legislative Route: A Summary and Conclusion

Public lands use, conservation, and environmental protection are intertwined in a complex web of government policies. Preservation of native species and economic exploitation of the public domain have co-existed for much of our history. All are central preoccupations of select congressional committees, and at times, the membership of both chambers. Land use regulation and property rights are not incompatible ideas, although some might speak of them as such. Indeed, this chapter demonstrates how Congress has balanced the two since the Second World War. That said, it appears that the emphasis on the economic uses of the public domain was softened somewhat by the entry of environmental and conservation concerns after 1970. By the mid-1970s these concerns were institutionalized in Congress, with specific committees charged with oversight of the various laws that constituted the basis of an environmental protection and species conservation regime. The success of the environmental movement sparked a counter-mobilization, that to date has realized only limited success in Congress.

Despite their failure to see taking legislation enacted into law, the proponents of property rights were able to claim small legislative victories in the GOP controlled House. While the property rights crowd achieved a precarious toehold on the congressional agenda following the victory of the GOP in 1994, it is far from clear that the property rights interpretation of the issue is the dominant view on the congressional agenda. Indeed, the lack of legislative success in the Senate, and the reluctance of the Bush administration to back taking legislation, counsels against any suggestion that the property rights proponents have won the battle for agenda control.

Congress's refusal to enact limits or prohibitions against regulatory taking is in part due to the ability of opponents to highlight the potentially sweeping impact of such limitations, especially the fiscal effects. In 1985 the federal government paid $23 million in compensation to taking challenges, $5.5 million in 1986, and $20.2 million in 1987. One year after the *Nollan* and *First English* Supreme Court decisions, the federal government had more than $1 billion in taking claims pending against it (Wise 1992). As a result of the potential high costs of takings legislation, the American public could face an enormous tax burden to pay off the claims, which even one of the sponsors of property rights legislation, Billy Tauzin (R-LA), admits would "bankrupt the government" (Byrnes 1995).

The truth be told, it is also obvious to many that the property rights movement targets environmental, land use, and reclamation regulation for the brunt of their ire. Opponents of property rights legislation have successfully argued that the TIA process would severely weaken or even repeal environmental, conservation, and public health and safety laws, thus hampering the ability for government to protect the public interest (Moulton 1995). This, combined with the concerns of state and municipal governments charged with much of land use planning, that takings legislation would make it impossible for them to do their jobs, severely limits the number of congressional allies.

Perhaps more important, our study indicates that the public lands policy subsystem has reached a détente of sorts with the environmental policy subsystem. This means the cries of an out of control regulatory state fall on deaf ears in Congress, even among those members who share no love for regulation. The public lands subsystem has made its peace with environmental regulation long ago (not that they may not revisit the issue on occasion). This is the way Congress works, through mutual accommodation of the needs of members, the political parties, and clientele. The problem facing property rights interests is that they have failed to establish an institutional basis or venue from which to base their demands. It appeared, for a brief moment, that the GOP would provide them with an "in" as part of the Contract With America. But, as was the case with most CWA legislation passed in House, the property rights legislation foundered in the Senate. The failure of CWA legislation to make it through the Senate can be attributed, in part, to the way Speaker Gingrich rammed it through the House. In choosing to bypass the standing committees, he not only shortened his speakership, but also set off alarm bells in the Senate. Quite simply, strong- arm tactics are no substitute for an institutional base of power like a committee. Not only that, in bypassing the committees Gingrich was attempting an end around the various policy subsystems, a feat most presidents are unable to accomplish, let alone a speaker in his first year. Finally, there was just no broad-base or institutional support for the property rights position in either chamber. The Judiciary Committees appear to be the most sympathetic venue, especially in the Senate when Orrin Hatch (R-Ut) chaired the committee, but even then the support constituted only a minority. So in the end, takings proponents were left with nowhere to turn but the states, a subject to which we turn in our final chapter.

CHAPTER SIX

If at First you do not Succeed...

Previous chapters focused on the Supreme Court and Congress as venues in the effort to set the property rights agenda. While property rights interests have recently enjoyed limited success in each venue, they have failed to establish control over either agenda, nor have they defined the issue to their liking. This chapter concludes our study with a brief exploration of the effort to shift the dynamic of setting the property rights agenda to the states. The effort to move the discussion from the federal venues to state legislatures represents a vertical shift in the process of agenda setting (Baumgartner and Jones 1993, 34). What we cannot do in the space of this conclusion is prove there was an effort on the part of the property rights community to move the regulatory takings issue out of the federal venues to the states. Rather, we simply document the shift, explore explanations for it, and offer some concluding observations based on interviews and other studies.

Taking it to the states

A venue shift has occurred regarding property rights in the last decade. Table 6 documents the venue shift by providing a timeline of the major policy events regarding property rights. Table 6 illustrates how the Supreme Court and Congress were the primary venues considering the takings issue prior to 1991. The property rights issue shifts to the states in 1991, when Washington enacted state level takings assessment legislation. Since 1991 state legislatures have been a virtual industry of takings legislation. The states' actions would seem to indicate a vertical shift in the process of agenda setting. The explanation behind this shift can be found in the failure of other venues to provide a solution to the liking of property rights advocates.

Chapter four documented the Supreme Court's refusal to provide categorical criteria to be used in settling the takings issue. Instead, the Court prefers an ad hoc approach in defining what type of government activity constitutes a taking and the circumstances surrounding compensation. While the Court has set a base line of sorts in *Lucas*, a regulatory taking that deprives an owner of all "economically viable" use of their property must be compensated, they have failed to establish categorical standards governing partial takings. The Court's thinking on the matter has evolved, or at least varied, among a variety of standards—the "too far" edict, the "bundle of property rights" approach, and the "essential nexus" condition, have all figured into the Court's thinking at one time or another. In the end, the Court has been most comfortable with settling cases on an ad-hoc, case-by-case basis. Therefore, despite the efforts of the property rights movement to use the judicial venue to resolve the regulatory takings issue, takings jurisprudence is still fairly amorphous.

Congress, too, has proven a disappointment to property rights advocates seeking to enshrine their definition of takings in law (see chapter five). Property rights advocates explain their inability to succeed in the congressional venue as the product of a combination of factors ranging from a cultural divide in the country that is magnified in Congress, to the role of entrenched interests who block all change. Myron Ebell, of Frontiers of Freedom, argues the split between urban and rural America is being played out in the debates over takings. "Urban representatives think they know what is best for the environment, and rural Americans, who own and work the land, feel they know what is best, not government" (Ebell 1999). In conflating urban representatives with "government" and rural interests with "the people," Ebell is resurrecting an imagery (and division) as old as the Republic. In this view, environmental regulation, a product of a government controlled by urban interests, is diametrically opposed to the interests of rural (agricultural) America. In Ebell's view, this division is magnified because urban legislators can erect institutional roadblocks to takings legislation. The congressional inability to pass takings legislation can be explained by the entrenched interests who free-ride on environmental, species protection, and land use regulation. "Lots of people are getting something for free—that is, the use of land—so they have a vested interest to stop property rights bills"(Ebell 1999).

Echoing the sentiment of many in the property rights camp, Larry Block, senior counsel for the Senate Judiciary Committee, commented that the property rights issue in the Senate demonstrates that chamber's philosophical division between Democrats and Republicans regarding the role of regulation. He suggests that "the Democrats favor regulation, and the Republicans want laissez faire capitalism." Since the Democrats view the property rights bills as an attack on the government's right and ability to regulate the economy, they oppose them (Block 1999).

A second explanation for congressional inaction involves the character of the property rights movement itself. Members from the various property rights groups agree that the movement has not matured enough to significantly influence policy at the federal level. Maturity in this context refers to organization and command of resources. Michael Wasylik, of Defenders of Property Rights, admits that the movement is "too young, disorganized, and small." And, although they claim there are over 1200 property rights groups and land use groups in America, property rights advocates have proven unable to assemble them into an effective peak association. Myron Ebell, of Frontiers of Freedom, suggests this is because "a lot of them are fighting local, specific issues" and lack the time and resources to move on the national front (Ebell 1999).

According to Wasylik, the movement's immaturity and disorganization has two important implications for its success in influencing policy. First, the movement's disorganization has prevented it from communicating its stance on property rights sufficiently. Therefore, "the federal legislators do not see the broad support out there that they prefer, and that [would make] them comfortable in passing takings legislation" (Wasylik 1999). Second, the movement's fragmentation makes it difficult to organize nationally because "people normally do not get involved until their property is effected" (Ebell 1999). In this view, the lack of success in the congressional venue is a problem of organization and attention to the issue. The solution, appears simple, raise public attention. Ebell (1999), however, admits that "it is hard to get media sympathy for [wealthy] property owners, while it is easy to get sympathy for poor people when their rights are violated."

The lack of success in federal venues appears to have contributed to the concentration of efforts at the state level. Table 6 traces the evolution of the takings issue as it bounces between venues. As is often the case, propertied interests began their challenge in the Court, where they were initially rebuffed. Following that first opinion in *Mugler*, property rights advocates enjoyed a series of small wins over the course of the twentieth century. As was recounted in the third chapter, property rights advocates begin to work the congressional venue in the 1970s, following the creation of an environmental protection regime. The issue bounces between these two federal venues for the next decade and a half, when the state of Washington becomes the first to adopt takings legislation.

Since 1991, twenty states have adopted some type of takings legislation, and every state but Connecticut has considered takings legislation. Table 6 indicates the year and type of takings legislation enacted by each state.[14] Washington enacted the first state takings legislation in

1991, only to have it rejected by a 3-2 margin in a public vote on a 1995 ballot referendum (Carson 1996). Arizona and Delaware enacted takings legislation in 1992, although Arizona's bill was later rejected by a 60/40 margin in a public vote on a 1994 ballot referendum. In 1993, Indiana and Utah enacted takings legislation, and thirty states considered approximately sixty-five takings bills. In 1994, Idaho, Mississippi, Missouri, Tennessee, Utah, and West Virginia enacted takings legislation, while thirty-one states considered approximately seventy takings bills. In 1995, Arizona, Florida, Idaho, Kansas, Louisiana, Mississippi, Montana, North Dakota, Texas, Virginia, and Wyoming enacted takings legislation. This was also the high point of the issue at the state level, with some form of takings legislation introduced in forty states. In 1996, Maine and Michigan enacted takings legislation, while twenty-nine states considered similar legislation. Idaho enacted takings legislation in 1998, followed by Oregon's Measure 7, adopted by voters by a margin of 53 percent to 47 percent in 2001 (Echeverria 2001).

For the most part, state-level takings legislation is of the assessment type. As such, it is largely symbolic, and is best understood as an "attempt to reinforce the constitutional requirements [in place], not to redefine them" (Echeverria 2001, 7). Mark Cordes (1997) suggests there are three variations of assessment statutes. The first category considers the assessment process used and the degree of administrative burden imposed on state agencies. In Indiana and Delaware the attorney general decides if agency rules are in compliance, while in Idaho, Michigan, and Tennessee, the agencies make their own informal determinations pursuant to attorney general guidelines.[15] Kansas, Louisiana, Montana, North Dakota, Texas, Utah,

If at First you do not Succeed

and West Virginia require the state agency to prepare a formal written analysis that must include assessments of

Table 6.1 Venue Shifting

Year	Supreme Court	Congress	State Law
1887	*Mugler v Kansas* Court refuses to find takings for regulations that serve a significant public purpose		
1915	*Hadacheck v Sebastian*		
1922	*Pennsylvania Coal v Mahon* "too far" definition adopted		
1978	*Pennsylvania Coal Transportation Co v NY* "investment-backed expectations" enters the taking lexicon	6 bills introduced in House	
1979		7 bills introduced in House 1 bill introduced in Senate Senate hearing on relocation assistance	
1981		Senate introduces and passes relocation assistance 4 bills introduced in House, none are acted on	
1983		Senate introduces and passes relocation assistance 5 bills introduced in House, none are acted on	
1985		House bill to amend the interest provisions of the Taking Act signed into law Senate passes relocation assistance	

Year	Court Case	Executive/Legislative	States
1987	*Keystone Bituminous Coal Assoc v DeBenedictus* "bundle of rights" concept *First Evangelical Lutheran Church v Los Angeles* "temporary takings" require compensation *Nollan v California Coastal Commission* "essential nexus"		
1988	*Agins v City of Tiburon* 2 part test developed	President Reagan issues EO 12630	
1991		4 bills seeking to enshrine EO 12630 into law introduced in House	Wa (TA)
1992	*Lucas v South Carolina* "all economically viable use"		Az (TA), De (TA)
1993			In (TA), Ut (TA)
1994	*Dolan v City of Tigard* Agins test reaffirmed		Id (TA), Ms (TC), Mo (TA), Tn (TA), WV (TA)
1995		House passes CWA takings legislation	Fl (TA), Ks (TA), La (TA, TC), Mt(TA), ND(TA), Tx (TA,TC), Va (TA), Wy (TA)
1996			Me (TA), Mi (TA)
1997	*Suitum v Tahoe Regional Planning* "ripeness" redefined	House passes takings legislation	
1998			Id (TC)
1999	*City of Monterey v Del Monte Dunes* establishes a right to jury trial and ripeness redefined		
2000			Or (TC)
2001	*Palazzolo v Rhode Island* Ripeness revisited	House passes takings legislation	
2002	*Tahoe-Sierra Preservation Council v TRPA* temporary moratoria examined		

TA-Takings Assessment; TC-Takings Compensation

alternative actions that might have less impact on property rights.[16] In addition, Louisiana, Montana, North Dakota, and West Virginia require an estimate of the cost of compensation and the source of payment.[17] Finally, Kansas, Utah, West Virginia, Louisiana, and North Dakota require that the assessment contain an affirmative justification for the restriction (Cordes 1997).[18]

The second category of assessment statutes considers their scope, meaning the range of government bodies subject to the assessment requirement and the types of actions that must be assessed. West Virginia and Michigan limit the assessment process to select state agencies.[19] Whereas, Delaware, Kansas, Montana, North Dakota, Tennessee, and Utah impose their requirements on all state agencies, but not their political subdivisions.[20] Finally, Idaho, Texas, and Louisiana, include both state agencies and all or most local governments (Cordes 1997).[21]

The final category of assessment statutes considers whether the legislation creates any additional duties subject to judicial review. Idaho, Kansas, and Washington discourage judicial review of the assessments.[22] Delaware and Texas require limited judicial review (Delaware to ensure that the attorney general has reviewed the rule in question and Texas for voiding the action, but only if no assessment has been prepared).[23] Other states have no definite rule.

Louisiana, Mississippi, Florida, Texas and Oregon have enacted legislation that goes beyond assessment and the current constitutional understanding of a takings (Eceverria 2001). Their compensation statutes provide monetary relief to adversely affected landowners once the diminution in value as a result of a regulatory taking reaches a defined threshold. The greatest variation within compensation statutes pertains to the threshold at which a percentage diminution in value triggers the requirement for compensation. The Mississippi statute requires that compensation be paid for regulation of agriculture and forest land causing a 40 percent or greater loss in value.[24] Louisiana's similar law is triggered by a 20 percent diminution.[25] Note that both statutes only apply to agricultural and forest lands, although the diminution in value criteria applies to any portion of the property (Echeverria 2001, 8). To date, it does not appear any claims have been filed under either act (Echeverria 2001, 10).

The Texas statute pertains to any property, and requires government compensation when governmental action reduces the property value by 25 percent or more.[26] The Texas act also requires government agencies to file takings impact assessments if their actions are likely to result in a taking. The act exempts municipalities, for the most part, and does not provide authority for property owners to sue for monetary relief (Echeverria 2001, 10). The Texas Supreme Court has agreed to hear on appeal a case dealing with water use and the ESA. As Echeverria (2001, 11) surmises, "The Court's decision could help consign the Texas takings act to continued relative obscurity. Or it could convert the act into a major weapon for challenging state rules and regulations." One commonality among the Mississippi, Louisiana, and Texas compensation laws is that they preclude compensation where the proscribed use constituted a common law nuisance.

Florida's "Bert J. Harris, Jr., Private Property Rights Protection Act" and Idaho's "Protection of Real Property Rights" bill do not set a percentage diminution. Instead, they require compensation when a government action "inordinately burdens" (Florida) or "unreasonably burdens" (Idaho) real property use (Cordes 1997).[27] The states define the two concepts similarly, as meaning either that the land owner is "permanently unable to attain the reasonable investment-backed expectations" for the property, or that an owner "bears permanently a disproportionate share of a burden imposed for the good of the public, which in fairness should be born by the public at large" (Cordes 1997).[28] While the Florida statute appears to be an attempt to apply the *Penn Central* standards, it goes on to define "existing use" in such a fashion that its application goes beyond current Court understanding of the term (Echeverria 2001, 12).

Oregon's Measure 7, unlike the preceding, applies retroactively to "essentially all uses of real property" (Echeverria 2001, 13). Under challenge in the Oregon Supreme Court, if it is upheld it will provide the right to claim monetary redress whenever regulation "has the effect of reducing the value of a property upon which the restriction is imposed" (Echeverria 2001, 1).

Explaining the Move to the States

In summary, twenty states have enacted some form of taking legislation. Still, it is far from evident that the shift of venue was orchestrated by those who claim to speak for the property rights forces. Indeed, given the lack of an authoritative national voice for the collection of disparate interests that consider themselves advocates of property rights, the shift appears to be the logical result of events that were always, at their heart, about local politics. That is, the concern over land use regulation is ultimately a local concern. While those on the losing side of any policy debate have an incentive to search for a more favorable venue for reconsideration of the issue (Baumgartner and Jones 1993; King 1991, 1992; Worsham 1997, 1998), the reality of the takings successes at the state level is a bit more complex, or muddled, than a simple vertical shift of venue orchestrated by property rights advocates.

Indeed, as much as they might like to, none of our respondents claimed responsibility for moving the issue from the federal level to the states. In their view, the vertical shift that occurred was not the result of coordinated strategic behavior by the property rights community, but rather a natural move by interests that are primarily local. Judy Brown, legislative assistant to the U.S. Chamber of Commerce, maintains that "the Chamber had no national directive to shift the issue (takings) to the states" (Brown 1999). Similarly, Larry Block suggests that by its very nature property rights is a "local issue, not a federal issue ... [and] it is inevitable that the states are going to rush to solve the issue" (Block 1999). In fact, Ron Arnold, of the Center for the Defense of Free Enterprise, argues "there is not a strategy to devolve the issue, nor to take [the] focus off Congress. ...[B]ut to keep pressure on the federal government to the point that all types of government are covered by federal property rights legislation" (Arnold 1999).

That said, we have not studied this aspect of the issue in sufficient detail to rule out that at least some national level economic interests might be behind the state level campaigns to limit state level regulation of land use. Indeed, the suggestion of Cody Lyons of the American Farm Bureau that "states have acted because the state legislators are in tune with what is needed locally" (Lyons 1999), suggests the influence and thinking of at least one peak association on the takings issue. There is little doubt that some state level government officials "see the problem and are sympathetic" to the concerns of property owners (Ebell 1999). While Myron Ebell, of Frontiers of Freedom, suggests that state legislators are more sympathetic to property rights concerns because they are not "captives" of national-level environmental interest groups, what goes unsaid is that the same state legislators are captured by local economic interests. An conclusion supported by a study of state level takings policy that found that representatives of the agriculture industry and business groups were instrumental in writing and passing takings legislation in Georgia, Indiana, and West Virginia (Moffett 1996).

It is no secret that the influence of environmental groups varies from state to state, and from the state level to the national level. In a study designed to determine the reasons for state level success or failure in passing takings legislation, Randy Moffett (1996) surveyed forty-five organizations—including agricultural and extractive industry associations, business associations, unions, grassroots citizens' property rights groups, state environmental organizations, and national citizen action and environmental groups—in Georgia, Indiana, New York, and West Virginia. He found that economic-based organizations enjoyed a distinct advantage over state environmental groups in those states that enacted takings legislation. He also found that the proponents of property rights considered their influence among state legislators to have increased after the 1994 state elections. The data in Table 6.1 supports this claim, fifteen of the twenty states with takings legislation on the books in 1999 enacted it after 1994. Indeed, table 6.1 suggests that while property interests have not abandoned either federal venue, they have become increasingly active in the states. True, much of the legislation is symbolic. But symbolic or not, it establishes a niche for the property rights advocates definition of the issue.

Conclusion

Clearly, the property rights issue has undergone a vertical shift in venue, so that it is now contested in multiple venues at both the state and federal level. That said, it does not appear that the issue itself resonates among a large segment of the public. It is given little sustained attention in the press and there is little evidence of a nationwide mass movement. Rather, interest in the issue appears to be sporadic and mostly regional with a definite local tilt. That is, the right to property resonates in pockets of the country for brief periods, as evident by the rise and fall of the Sagebrush rebellion and the Wise Use movements, and even in those regions that it resonates, it is often a localized concern. What this means in terms of agenda setting is that property rights advocates appear to have given up on an outside initiative approach at the national level. Instead, they have counted on a few policy entrepreneurs in Congress who employ a combination of inside initiative and mobilization, in an effort to keep the issue on the House and Senate agendas. The high point of the mobilization efforts to date was the inclusion of property rights legislation in the bundle of measures passed in the House as part of the Contract With America.

If ever a window of opportunity presented itself, it was the election of the GOP House in 1994, hard on the heels of several favorable property rights rulings in a Supreme Court dominated by GOP appointed justices. Yet in the end, House efforts went nowhere, in part because of presidential objections, but also because some members of the Senate took to heart the objections of state level officials.

The result is that the Court has continued in its incremental ratification of a property rights reading of the Constitution, reluctant to redefine the issue completely, but increasingly sympathetic to an interpretation that would greatly limit the application of land use regulations. That said, the Court's 5-4 breakdown on most takings cases suggests the past pattern could be easily reversed.

Finally, while we have made reference to the property rights movement, there is less there than meets the eye, or perhaps more. That is, while several policy entrepreneurs speak in terms of a movement, often claim to lead a group with members too numerous to count, and wrap themselves in the language of political movements, there does not appear to be a well organized, membership based organization that would fit the standard definition of a political movement. This is not to say that there are not advocacy groups, think tanks, and legal foundations devoted to the takings issue and a property rights ideal. But they are far from constituting a rebellion, movement, or mass-based interest group. Instead of a movement one finds foundations with and without corporate sponsors, self-published ideologues, disgruntled property owners, real estate developers, agricultural interests, and the like, whose involvement in and commitment to some property rights ideal varies over time. In short, a wide variety of interests, who think and act in both broad and narrow terms, are involved at various levels of government with the issue of regulating the use of property. In the end, we are left to conclude that the takings issue is in no danger of being resolved to the satisfaction of any particular interest any time soon.

APPENDIX

Title	Bill #	Type[a]	Date[b]	Sponsor	Referral Comm.(s)	Final Action
			95th Congress, 1977-1978			
Big Thicket National Preserve Act	H.R.2544	EDC	1/26/77	Wilson, C.H.	Interior and Insular Affairs	
Joint Resolution to designate the third week in April each year as "National Private Property Week"	H.J.Res.261	S	2/16/77	Spellman	Post Office and Civil Service	
Bill to provide reimbursement... to real property owners... of litigation expenses arising from the condemnation of real property,... by the National Park Service	H.R.8215	EDC	7/12/77	Brodhead	HGovernment Operations Public Works and Transportation	
Bill to Amend the Uniform Relocation Assistance and Real Property Acquisition Policies Act of 1970	H.R.9387	EDC	9/30/77	Andrews	Public Works and Transportation	
Bill to Amend the Uniform Relocation Assistance and Real Property Acquisition Policies Act of 1970	H.R.9772	EDC	10/27/77	Andrews	Public Works and Transportation	
Bill to Amend the Uniform Relocation Assistance and Real Property Acquisition Policies Act of 1970	H.R.10122	EDC	11/29/77	Andrews	Public Works and Transportation	

Title	Bill #	Type[a]	Date[b]	Sponsor	Referral Comm.(s)	Final Action
Uniform Relocation Assistance Act Amendments of 1979	S.1108	EDC	5/9/79	Sasser	Governmental Affairs	
96th Congress, 1979-1980						
Bill to acquire certain lands ... preservation and protection of the Potomac River Shoreline	H.R.4947	EDC	7/24/79	Stark	District of Columbia	
Uniform Relocation Assistance Act Amendments of 1980	H.R.6256	EDC	1/22/80	Schroeder	Public Works and Transportation	
Uniform Relocation Assistance Act Amendments of 1980	H.R.6463	EDC	2/7/80	Mineta	Public Works and Transportation	
Uniform Relocation Assistance Act Amendments of 1979	H.R.6756	EDC	3/10/80	Wolff	Public Works and Transportation	
Bill to Amend the Uniform Relocation Assistance and Real Property Acquisition Policies Act of 1970	H.R.8141	EDA	9/17/80	Ullman	Public Works and Transportation	Executive statement requested from DOT, GSA, Interior, OMB.
Bill to Amend the Uniform Relocation Assistance and Real Property Acquisition Policies Act of 1970	H.R.8208	EDC	9/24/80	Volkmer	Public Works and Transportation	
Compensate individuals for land taken ... Act of 1964	H.R.8304	EDC	10/2/80	Roybal	Judiciary	
97th Congress, 1981-1982						
Uniform Relocation Asstnce Act Amendments of 1981	S.2363	EDC	4/13/82	Durenberger	Governmental Affairs	Passed Senate (8/5/82)

Title	Bill #	Type[a]	Date[b]	Sponsor	Referral Comm.(s)	Final Action
Bill for the relief of the prior owners of the Harris Neck Wildlife Refuge, or their heirs	H.R.1044	EDC	1/22/81	Ginn	Judiciary	
Uniform Relocation Assistance Act Amendments of 1981	H.R.1529	EDC	2/2/81	Edwards	Public Works and Transportation	
Bill to Amend the Federal Rules of Civil Procedure	H.R.3691	EDC	5/21/81	Whitten	Judiciary	
Uniform Relocation Assistance and Real Property Acquisition Policies Act Amendments of 1982	H.R.6171	EDC	4/27/82	Howard	Public Works and Transportation	
98th Congress, 1983-1984						
Uniform Relocation Act Amendments of 1983	S.531	EDC	2/17/83	Durenberger	Governmental Affairs Public Works and Transportation	Passed Senate (5/20/83) and referred to House Subcom on Surface Transportation
Bill to Amend the Uniform Relocation Assistance and Real Property Acquisition Policies Act of 1970	H.R.1687	EDC	2/25/83	Howard	Public Works and Transportation	
Bill to Amend the Federal Rules of Civil Procedure	H.R.1828	EDC	3/2/83	Whitten	Judiciary	
Bill to compensate... ranchers for ranching units taken by the Department of the Army for the White Sands Missile Range, NM	H.R.4022	EDC	9/28/83	Skeen	Judiciary	

Title	Bill#	Type[a]	Date[b]	Sponsor	Referral Comm.(s)	Final Action
Bill to restore the right to a jury trial in certain cases involving the exercise by the government of the power of eminent domain	H.R.6107	EDC	8/8/84	Whitten	Judiciary	
Bill to restore the right to a jury trial in certain cases involving the exercise by the government of the power of eminent domain	H.R.6127	EDC	8/9/84	Whitten	Judiciary	
99th Congress, 1985-1986						
Uniform Relocation Act Amendments of 1985	S.249	EDC	1/22/85	Durenberger	Governmental Affairs	Passed Senate
Bill to amend the interest provisions of the Declaration of Taking Act	S.2424	EDC	5/8/86	Thurmond	Judiciary	Indefinitely postponed by Senate
Declaration of Taking Amendments Act of 1986	H.R.4586	EDC	4/15/86	Fish	Judiciary	
Bill to amend the interest provisions of the Declaration of Taking Act	H.R.5363	EDC	11/14/86	Glickman	Judiciary	Became Public Law No: 99-656
101st Congress, 1989-1990						
White Sands Fair Compensation Act of 1989	S.1725	EDC	10/4/89	Domenici	Judiciary	
White Sands Fair Compensation Act of 1989	H.R.3408	EDC	10/4/89	Skeen	Judiciary	

Title	Bill#	Type[a]	Date[b]	Sponsor	Referral Comm.(s)	Final Action
			102nd Congress, 1991-1992			
Private Property Rights Act of 1991	S.50	TA	1/14/91	Symms	Governmental Affairs	
White Sands Fair Compensation Act of 1991	S.867	EDC	4/18/91	Domenici	Energy and Natural Resources	
Property Rights Act of 1991	H.R.905	TA	2/6/91	McEwen	Government Operations Judiciary	
Private Property Rights Act of 1991	H.R.1572	TA	3/21/91	Olin	Agriculture	
Private Property Rights Act of 1991	H.R.1650	TA	3/22/91	Solomon	Judiciary	
Just Compensation Act of 1991	H.R.2185	TC	5/1/91	Smith, R.F.	Merchant Marine and Fisheries Public Works and Transportation Interior and Insular Affairs	
A Bill to Amend the Endangered Species Act	H.R.6123	TC	10/3/92	Thomas, W.	Merchant Marine and Fisheries	

Title	Bill#	Type[a]	Date[b]	Sponsor	Referral Comm.(s)	Final Action
			103rd Congress, 1993-1994			
A bill to ... avoid ... taking of private property	S. 177		1/21/93	Dole, R R-Ks 25 cosponsors	Governmental Affairs	
Private Property Owners Bill of Rights	S.1915	TC	3/9/94	Shelby R-Al	Environment and Public Works	
Private Property Rights Act of 1994	S.2006	TA	3/25/94	Dole R-Ks	Governmental Affairs	
Private Property Rights Restoration Act	S.2410	TC	8/19/94	Gramm R-Tx	Governmental Affairs	
Farm, Ranch, and Homestead Protection Act of 1994	S. 2451	TC	9/2294	Hutchinson R-Tx 1 cosponsor	Environment and Public Works	
Private Property Rights Act of 1993	H.R. 385		1/5/93	Solomon R-NY	Judiciary	
Private Property Protection Act of 1993	H.R. 561	TA	1/25/93	Condit D-Ca	Agriculture	
Just Compensation Act of 1993	H.R. 1388	TC	3/17/93	Smith, R 111 cosponsors	Natural Resources	
A bill to compensate owners of property substantially diminished in value as a consequence of a final decision of any United States agency	H.R.3784	TC	2/2/94	Smith, L 3 cosponsors	Judiciary	Referred to House Judiciary

Title	Bill#	Type[a]	Date[b]	Sponsor	Referral Comm.(s)	Final Action
Private Property Owners Bill of Rights	H.R.3875	TC	2/23/94	Tauzin R-La 171 cosponsors	Merchant Marine and Fisheries Public Works and Transportation Judiciary	Unfavorable Executive Comment received from Justice Referred to House Public Works
Private Property Rights Act of 1994	H.R.4418	TA	5/12/94	Roberts R-Ks	Government Operations Judiciary	
104th Congress, 1995-1996						
Private Property Rights Act of 1995	S.22	TA	1/4/95	Dole R-Ks 12 cosponsors	Governmental Affairs	
Regulatory Accountability Act of 1995	S. 100	TA	1/4/95	Glenn D-Oh	Governmental Affairs	
Property Rights Litigation Relief Act of 1995	S.135	TC	1/4/95	Hatch R-Ut	Judiciary	
Private Property Rights Restoration Act of 1995	S.145	TC	1/4/95	Gramm R-Tx 13 cosponsors	Governmental Affairs	
Private Property Owners Bill of Rights	S.239	TC	1/18/95	Shelby R-Al 11 cosponsors	Governmental Affairs	
Comprehensive Wetlands Conservation and Management Act of 1995	S. 352	TC	2/3/95	Pressler, L	Environment and Public Works	

Title	Bill#	Type[a]	Date[b]	Sponsor	Referral Comm.(s)	Final Action
Omnibus Property Rights Act of 1995	S.605	TC	3/23/95	Dole R-Ks 33 cosponsors	Judiciary	
Endangered Species Act Reform Act of 1995	S.768	TC	5/9/95	Gorton R-Wa	Environment and Public Works	
Omnibus Property Rights Act of 1996	S.1954	TC	7/16/96	Hatch R-Ut 34 cosponsors	Judiciary	Reported to Senate and placed on legislative calendar
Private Property Protection Act of 1995	H.R.130	TA	1/4/95	Solomon R-NY 2 cosponsors	Judiciary Agriculture	
Property Rights Litigation Relief Act of 1995	H.R.489	TC	1/11/95	Smith, L 28 cosponsors	Judiciary	Second reading in Senate and placed on legislative calendar
Farm, Ranch, and Homestead Protection Act of 1995	H.R. 590	TC	1/11/95	Smith, L 20 cosponsors	Resources	
Private Property Owners Bill of Rights	H.R. 790	TA/TC	2/1/95	Tauzin R-LA 88 cosponsors	Judiciary Resources Transportation & Infrastructure	
Private Property Protection Act of 1995	H.R.925	TC	2/14/95	Canady	Judiciary Environment and Public Works	
Comprehensive Wetlands Conservation and Management Act of 1995	H.R. 1268	TC	3/21/95	English 1 cosponsor	Transportation & Infrastructure	

Title	Bill#	Type[a]	Date[b]	Sponsor	Referral Comm.(s)	Final Action
Private Property Impact Assessment Act of 1995	H.R.1277	TA	3/21/95	Condit D-Ca	Judiciary Agriculture	Passed House (3/3/95) and referred to Senate Environment and Public Works Committee
Comprehensive Wetlands Conservation and Management Act of 1995	H.R. 1330	TC	3/28/95	Hayes, JA 59 cosponsors	Transportation & Infrastructure	
American Land Sovereignty Protection Act of 1996	H.R.3752	EDA	6/27/96	Young R-Alaska	Resources	
105th Congress, 1997-1998						
Bill to Amend the National Wildlife Refuge System Administration Act of 1966	S.491	EDA	3/20/97	Ford R-Ky	Environment and Public Works	Failed Passage in House (9/26/96)
Private Property Rights Act of 1997	S.709	TA	5/7/97	Hagel R-Nb 3 cosponsors	Governmental Affairs	
Omnibus Property Rights Act of 1997	S. 781	TA/TC	5/22/97	Hatch R-Ut 18 cosponsors	Judiciary	
Private Property Owners Bill of Rights	S.953	TC	6/24/97	Shelby R-Al 4 cosponsors	Governmental Affairs	
Property Owners Access to Justice Act of 1997	S.1204	EDA	9/23/97	Coverdell R-Ga 31 cosponsors	Judiciary	
Citizens Access to Justice Act of 1997	S.1256	EDA	10/6/97	Hatch R-Ut 1 cosponsor	Judiciary	

Title	Bill#	Type[a]	Date[b]	Sponsor	Referral Comm.(s)	Final Action
Property Rights Implementation Act of 1998	S.2271	EDA TC	7/7/98	Hatch R-Ut 2 cosponsors	Judiciary	
Private Property Protection Act of 1997	H.R.95	TA	1/7/97	Solomon R-NY	Judiciary Agriculture	
Private Property Rights Implementation Act of 1997	H.R.1534	TA	5/6/97	Gallegly 239 cosponsors	Judiciary Judiciary	Cloture on motion to proceed not invoked in Senate
Prompt Compensation Act of 1998	H.R. 4303	TA/TC	7/22/98	Hunter, D 10 cosponsors	Judiciary	
Endangered Species Land Management Reform Act	H.R.4554	TC	9/11/98	Thomas	Resources	Passed House (10/22/97)
106th Congress, 1999-2000						
Private Property Rights act of 1999	S. 246	TA/TC	1/19/99	Hagel C R-Nb 2 cosponsors	Governmental Affairs	
Citizens Access to Justice Act of 1999	S. 1028		5/13/99	Hatch R-Ut 18 cosponsors	Judiciary	
Private Property Protection Act of 1999	H.R. 294	TA	1/6/99	Sweeney, J	Judiciary Agriculture	
Prompt Compensation Act of 1999	H.R. 1002	TC	3/16/99	Hunter, D 17 cosponsors	Judiciary	
Landowners Equal Treatment Act of 1999	H.R. 1142	TC	3/17/99	Young, D R-Alaska 63 cosponsors	Resources	

Title	Bill#	Type[a]	Date[b]	Sponsor	Referral Comm.(s)	Final Action
Private Property Rights Implementation Act of 1999	H.R. 2372	TC	3/20/2000	Canady, T 112 cosponsors	Judiciary	
Private Property Protection Act of 1999	H.R. 2550	TC	3/27/2000	Delay R-Tx 37 cosponsors	Judiciary	Reported and placed on the calendar
107th Congress, 2001						
Private Property Rights Act of 2001	S.1412	TA/TC	9/10/01	Hagel R-Nb	Governmental Affairs	Passed House Referred to Senate Judiciary
Private Property Protection Act of 2001	H.R. 212	TA	1/3/01	Sweeney, J 1 cosponsor	Judiciary Agriculture	
Endangered Species Act Amendments	H.R 472	TC	2/6/01	Radanovich, G	Resources	
Endangered Species Land Management Reform Act	H.R. 1403	TC	4/4/01	Thomas, W 2 cosponsors	Resources	
Rural America Protection Act of 2001	H.R. 2719	EDC	8/2/01	Davis, JoAnn 2 cosponsors	Transportation & Infrastructure	

Source: Compiled from "Thomas: Legislative Information on the Internet." (http://thomas.loc.gov)

[a] Refers to the type of property rights legislation: S = symbolic; EDA = eminent domain assessment; EDC = eminent domain compensation; TA = takings assessment; and, TC = takings compensation.

[b] Refers to the date of introduction.

NOTES

1. This is a slight overstatement. There are ways of discharging a bill from committee. Still, their use is extremely rare and does not usually result in passage of the legislation (see Davidson and Oleszek 2002).

2. In conducting the search we used the terms eminent domain, mines and mining, mineral leases, public lands, right to property, regulatory taking, taking, wildlife. In addition we searched under any "see other" reference in the *Congressional Record*.

3. Graphing the House and Senate separately results in figures that closely mirror figure 5.1.

4. This includes their predecessors the Public Lands and Interior Committees.

5. The Baumgartner and Jones Agenda Project was made possible by a National Science Foundation grant, number SBR 9320922. The data is available from the Center for American Politics and Public Policy at the University of Washington or from the Department of Political Science at Penn State University. Needless to say, neither the NSF nor Baumgartner and Jones bear any responsibility for the analysis reported here, although we will buy them a beer when we see them next for saving us untold hours in data collection.

6. Since the Herfindahl index does not identify which committees are actually holding hearings, it is an imperfect measure of competition. Imperfect because it does not recognize a shift in the identity of the dominant committee from one period to the next, or a shift in the identity of competitors from one session to the next. Still, in light of what the figures indicate in the case of public lands policy, the Herfindahl index score gives one a feel for the dominance, and variation in the dominance, of the Resources committees in each chamber.

7. We do not report the scores here for ease of presentation.

8. The search included the years for the 93rd and 94th congresses, 1973-1976, which produced no takings legislation. The search was conducted using *Thomas* and employing the following terms: eminent domain, right of property, regulatory takings, takings, wise use movement and any other see other category listed in the *Legislative Indexing Vocabulary* of *Thomas*.

9. Symbolic legislation was prohibited by the 103rd Congress as part of the GOP reforms intended to speed the legislative process (see Davidson and Oleszek 2002).

10. This is quite similar to the pre-rule making restrictions that the Reagan administration attempted to impose vis-à-vis Executive Order 12498 on all executive agencies.

11. Executive Order No. 12630, 3 C.F.R., section 554 (1989), reprinted as amended in 3 U.S.C., section 301 (Supp. 1995).

12. Representative Tauzin changed his party affiliation to the GOP in August 1995.

13. Other statutes included in the scope of H.R. 925 are Title XII of the Food Security Act of 1985, 16 U.S.C., p. 3801-3862 (1994); the Federal Land Management Policy Act, 43 U.S.C., p. 1701-1784 (1994); and Section 6 of the Forest and Rangeland Renewable Resources Planning Act of 1974, 16 U.S.C., pg. 1604.

14. Data concerning state takings legislation was gathered from a variety of sources. The Georgetown Environmental Law and Policy Institute maintains a website that tracks, among other things, state level takings legislation (www.gelpi.org). John D. Echeverria was kind enough to share his insights with us regarding state level takings. Data regarding the dates of adoption was gathered from "Takings Legislation in the 50 United States," at the Institute for Global Communications website (www.igc.apc.org/arin/states.html.).

15. Delaware Code Ann. tit. 29, p.605 (Supp. 1996); Indiana Code Ann. Section 4-22-2-32 (West Supp. 1996); Idaho Code, Section 67-8001 (1995); Michigan Legis. Serv. 101 (West); Tennessee Code Ann., p.12-1-201 to 203 (Supp. 1996).

16. Kansas Stat. Ann., p.77-701 (supp. 1995); Louisiana Rev. Stat. Ann., section 3:3609 (West Supp. 1997); Montana Code Ann., p.2-10-105 (1995); North Dakota Cent. Code, section 28-32-02.5 (Supp. 1995); Texas Gov't Code Ann., section 2007.043 (West 1996); Utah Code Ann., section 93-90-4 (Supp. 1996); West Virginia Code, section 22-1A-3 (1994).

17. Louisiana Rev. Stat. Ann., section 3:3609(B)(8), (9) (West Supp. 1997); Montana Code Ann., section 2-10-105(2)(C) (1995); North Dakota Cent. Code, section 28-32-02.5 (Supp. 1995); West Virginia Code, section 22-1A-3(a)(6) (1994).

18. Kansas Stat. Ann., section 77-706(1) Supp. 1995); Utah Code Ann., section 63-90-4 (Supp. 19960); West Virginia Code, section 22-1A-3(a)(1) (1994); Louisiana Rev. Stat. Ann., section 3:3699(B)(1) (West Supp. 1997); North Dakota Cent. Code, section 28-32-02.5(1)(b) (Supp. 1995).

19. West Virginia Code, section 22-1A-2 (1994); H.B. 4433, 88th Leg., Regular Sess. (Mich. 1995) (enacted).

20. Delaware Code Ann. tit. 29, p.605 (Supp. 1996); Kansas Stat. Ann., section 77-706(1) (Supp. 1995); Montana Code Ann., section 2-10-103(3) (1995); North Dakota Cent. Code, section 28-32-02.5(1) (Supp. 1995); Tennessee Code Ann., section 12-1-201 (Supp. 1996); Utah Code Ann., section 63-90-2-(4) (Supp. 1996).

21. Idaho Code, section 67-8003 (1995); Texas Gov't Code Ann., section 2007.042(a) (West 1996); Louisiana Stat. Ann., section 3:3602(13) (West Supp. 1997).

22. Idaho Code, section 67-8003 (1995); Kansas Stat. Ann., section 77-706(2) (supp. 1995); Washington Rev. Code, section 36.70A.370(4) (West Supp. 1997).

23. Delaware Code Ann. tit. 29, section 605(b) (Supp. 1996); Texas Govt Code, section 2007.044(a) (West 1996).

24. Mississippi Code Ann., Section 49-33-1 to 49-33-19 (Supp. 1996).

25. Louisiana Rev. Stat. Ann., Section 3:3601-02 (West Supp. 1997).

26. Texas Government Code, Section 2007.002.

27. Florida Stat. Ann., Sections 70.001(2), (3)(e) (West Supp. 1997); Idaho Code, Section 67: Chapter 84 (1998).

28. Florida Stat. Ann., Section 70.001(3)(e) (West Supp. 1997); Idaho Code, Section 67: Chapter 84(1) (1998).

REFERENCES

Aberbach, Joel D. 1990. *Keeping a Watchful Eye: The Politics of Congressional Oversight.* Washington D.C.: Brookings.

Alliance for America. 1998. Web site at http://www.allianceforamerica.org.

Alliance for Environment and Resources. 1998. Web site at http://www.cat.org.au/a4a/fake4.html

Alston, Dana. February 1, 1994. Interview with Mark Dowie, 1995.

Arnold, Ron. April 30, Telephone Interview.

Arrensen, David A. 1988. "Compensation for Regulatory Takings: Finality of Local Decisionmaking and the Measure of Compensation." *Indiana Law Journal.* 63:649-68.

Austin, Regina and Michael Schill. 1994. "Black, Brown, Red, and Poisoned," in *Unequal Protection*, ed. Robert Bullard. San Francisco: Sierra Club.

Bachrach, Peter, and Morton S. Baratz. 1962. "Two Faces of Power." *American Political Science Review.* 56:947-952.

Bast, Joseph, L., Peter J. Hill, and Richard C. Rue. 1994. *Eco-Sanity.* Lanham, M.D.: Madison Books.

Baumgartner, Frank R. and Bryan D. Jones. 1991. "Agenda Dynamics and Policy Subsystems." *Journal of Politics* 53:1044-74.

Baumgartner, Frank R. and Bryan D. Jones. 1993. *Agendas and Instability in American Politics.* Chicago: University of Chicago Press.

Baumgartner, Frank R., Bryan D. Jones and Michael C. Rosentiehl. 1997 "The Co-Evolution of Issues and Structures in Congress." Working Paper #2.

Center for American Politics and Public Policy, Department of Political Science, University of Washington.

Becker, Gary S. 1983. "A Theory of Competition among Pressure Groups for Political Influence." *Quarterly Journal of Economics*. 98:371-400.

Biskupic, Joan. 1994. "Justices Broaden Property Rights." *Washington Post*. June 25:A1.

Blaesser, Brian W., Clyde W. Forrest, Douglas W. Kmiec, Daniel R. Mandelker, Alan C. Weinstein, and Norman Williams, Jr. 1989. *Land Use and the Constitution*. Chicago: Planners Press.

Block, Larry. May 6, 1999. Telephone Interview.

Boeckelman, Keith. 1992. "The Influence of States on Federal Policy Adoptions." *Policy Studies Journal*. 20:365-375.

Bosso, Christopher J. 1987. *Pesticides and Politics: The Life Cycle of a Public Issue*. Pittsburgh: University of Pittsburgh Press.

Brick, Phil. 1995. "Determined Opposition: The Wise Use Movement Challenges Environmentalism." *Environment*. 37:8:17+.

Brisbin, Richard A. 1993. "Antonin Scalia, William Brennan, and the Politics of Expression." *American Political Science Review*. 87:912-927.

Brown, Judy. May 5, 1999. Telephone Interview.

Brown, William P. 1995. *Issues, Interests, and Places in a Postreform Congress: Agriculture's Policy Domain*. Lawrence: University Press of Kansas.

Bullard, Robert, ed. 1993. *Confronting Environmental Racism: Views from the Grassroots*. Boston: South End Press.

Butler, Lynda L. March 1997. "The Politics of Takings: Choosing the Appropriate Decisionmaker." *William and Mary Law Review*. 38:749-824.

Byrnes, Patricia. 1992. "The Counterfeit Crusade." *Wilderness*. 56(Summer): 29-31.

Byrnes, Patricia. 1995. "Are We Being Taken by Takings?" *Wilderness Watch*. 58(Spring):4-5.

Caldwell, Lynton. 1985. "Globalizing Environmentalism: Thresholds of a New Phase in International Relations." *Society and Natural Resources*. 4:259.

Carlin, Alan, Paul F. Scodari, and Don H. Garner. 1992. "Environmental Investments: The Costs of Cleaning Up." *Environment*. 34(March): 12-20, 38-44.

Carson, Ed. 1996. "Property Frights: Why Property Rights Initiatives Are Losing at the Polls." *Reason Magazine*. (May): 27-31.

Ceplo, Karol J. 1995. "Land-Rights Conflicts in the Regulation of Wetlands," in *Land Rights*, ed.Bruce Yandle. Lanham, M.D.: Rowman & Littlefield Publishers.

Chomski, Joseph M. and Constance E. Brooks. 1980. *The Sagebrush Rebellion: A ConciseAnalysis of the History, the Law and Politics of Public Land in the United States*. Alaska: Legislative Affairs Agency.

Clean Air Act. 42 U.S.C., 7401-7671q, (1988 and supp. 1991).

Cobb, Roger W. and Charles D. Elder. 1983. *Participation in American Politics: The Dynamics of Agenda Building*. Baltimore: John Hopkins University Press.

Cobb, Roger and Mark Howard Ross, eds. 1997. *Cultural Strategies of Agenda Denial:Avoidance, Attack and Redefinition*. Lawrence: University Press of Kansas.

Cobb, Roger, Jennie-Keith Ross, and Marc Howard Ross. 1976. "Agenda Building as a Comparative Political Process." *American Political Science Review.* 70:126-38.

Cohen, Michael, James March, and Johan Olsen. 1972. "A Garbage Can Model of Organizational Choice." *Administrative Science Quarterly.* 17:1-25.

Cordes, Mark W. 1997. "Leapfrogging the Constitution: The Rise of State Takings Legislation." *Ecology Law Quarterly.* 24:187-242.

Coyle, Marcia. 2001. "Landowners Win Rights to Attack Rules." *The National Law Journal.* (July 16)A1.

Delaney, John J. 1993. "Advancing Private Property Rights: the Lessons of Lucas." *Stetson Law Review.* 22:395-408.

DiGregorio, Christine. 1992. "Leadership Approaches in Congressional Committee Hearings." *Western Political Quarterly.* 45:971-83.

Downs, Anthony. 1972. "Up and Down With Ecology: The Issue Attention Cycle." *Public Interest.* 28:38-50

Dowie, Mark. 1995. *Losing Ground: American Environmentalism at the Close of the Twentieth Century.* Cambridge: MIT Press.

Dunlap, Riley E. 1987."Polls, Pollution, and Politics Revisited: Public Opinion on the Environment in the Reagan Era." *Environment.* 29: 32-37.

Dunlap, Thomas R. 1988. *Saving America's Wildlife.* Princeton: Princeton University Press.

Dunlap, Riley E. 1991. "Trends in Public Opinion." In Riley E. Dunlap and Angela G. Mertig, eds. *American Environmentalism: The US Environmental Movement, 1970-1990.* Philadelphia: Taylor and Francis.

Dunlap, Riley E. 1995. "Public Opinion and Environmental Policy," in James P. Lester, ed. *Environmental Politics and Policy: Theories and Evidence, 2nd ed.* Durham: Duke University Press.

Dye, Thomas. 1990. *American Federalism: Competition Among Governments.* Lexington, Mass.: Lexington Books.

Ebell, Myron. May 10, 1999. Telephone Interview.

Echeverria, John D. 2001. "Reflections on Oregon Measure 7." McCall Speakers Series, 1000 Friends of Oregon. Salem, Oregon, May 3.

Ehrlich, Paul. 1968. *The Population Bomb.* New York: Ballentine.

Eisenberg, Gary. 1988. "Property: The Takings Clause of the Fifth Amendment." *Annual Survey of American Law.* (September): 1105-1135.

Endangered Species Act. 1973. 16 U.S.C., p. 1532 (1988).

Epstein, Richard. 1985. *Takings: Private Property and the Power of Eminent Domain.* Cambridge, MA: Harvard University Press.

Eyestone, Robert. 1978. *From Social Issues to Public Policy.* New York: John Wiley and Sons.

Fellows, James A. 1996. "The Legal Doctrine of Regulatory Takings: An Evolving Issue." *The Appraisal Journal.* 64:363-374.

Fenno, Richard F. Jr. 1966. *The Power of the Purse: Appropriations Politics in Congress.* Boston: Little, Brown.

Fenno, Richard F. Jr. 1973. *Congressmen in Committees.* Boston: Little, Brown.

Freilich, Robert H. and Elizabeth A. Garvin. 1993. "Takings After *Lucas*: Growth Management, Planning, and Regulatory Implementation Will Work Better Than Before." *Stetson Law Review*, 22:409-434.

Froman, Lewis. 1967. *The Congressional Process: Styles, Rules and Procedures.* Boston: Little, Brown.

Gillroy, John M. and Robert Y. Shapiro. 1986. "The Polls: Environmental Protection." *Public Opinion Quarterly.* 50: 270-276.

Gottleib, Alan, ed. 1989. *The Wise Use Agenda.* Bellevue, WA.: Free Enterprise Press.

Greenhouse, Linda. 1992. "Justices Ease Way to Challenge Land-Use Rules That Prevent Development." *New York Times.* June 30: A18.

Greenhouse, Linda. 1994. "Revisiting Property Rights: Court Still Seems on the Fence." *New York Times.* March 24: A11.

Greider, William. 1992. *Who Will Tell the People: The Betrayal of American Democracy.* New York: Simon and Schuster.

Griffith, Ernest S. 1951. *Congress: Its Contemporary Role.* New York: New York University Press.

Hahn-Baker, David. 1994. "Rocky Roads to Consensus: Traditional Environmentalism Meets Environmental Justice." *Amicus Journal.* 16(Spring): 41-43.

Hall, Richard L. "Participation, Abdication, and Representation in Congressional Committees." In Lawrence C. Dodd and Bruce I. Oppenheimer. eds. *Congress Reconsidered.* 5th ed. Washington, DC: Congressional Quarterly.

Harris, Louis. 1989. "Public Worried About State of the Environment Today and in the Future." *Harris Poll.* 21: 1-4.

Harvard Law Review Association. 1999. "Leading Cases: I. Constitutional Law." *Harvard Law Review.* 113(November)296.

Harvard Law Review Association. 2001. "Leading Cases: I. Constitutional Law." *Harvard Law Review.* 115(November)447.

Hays, Samuel P. 1987. *Beauty, Health, and Permanence: Environmental Politics in the United States, 1955-1985.* Cambridge, England: Cambridge University Press.

Helvarg, David. 1994. "The Anti-Enviros Are Getting Uglier." *The Nation*. 259(November): 28.

Helvarg, David. 1994. *War Against the Greens: The "Wise Use Movement," The New Right, and Anti-Environmental Violence*. San Francisco: Sierra Books.

Higley, Charles J. 2000. "Takings: City of Monterey v. Del Monte Dunes." *Ecology Law Quarterly*. 27:603.

Hinckley, Barbara. 1971. *Stability and Change in Congress*. New York: Harper and Row.

Hoerner, Andrew J. 1995. "Life and Taxes." *The Amicus Journal*. Summer:14-17.

Holusha, John. 1988. "Bush Pledges Aid for Environment." *New York Times*, September 1.

Hopkins, Thomas D. 1991. *Cost of Regulation*. Rochester, New York: Rochester Institute of Technology.

Jones, Bryan D., Frank Baumgartner, and Jeffery C. Talbert. 1993a. "The Destruction of Issue Monopolies in Congress." *American Political Science Review* 87:657-71.

Jones, Bryan D., Frank Baumgartner, and Jeffery C. Talbert. 1993. *Agendas and Instability in American Politics*. Chicago: The University of Chicago Press.

Jones, Bryan. 1994. *Reconceiving Decision-Making in Democratic Politics*. Chicago: The University of Chicago Press.

Jones, Charles O., and Randall Strahan. 1985. "The Effect of Energy Politics on Congressional and Executive Organization in the 1970s." *Legislative Studies Quarterly*. 10:151-79.

Kanner, Gideon. 2001. "Temporary Takings." *The National Law Journal*. (November)A21.

Kelman, Steven. 1987. *Making Public Policy*. New York: Basic Books.

Kenworthy, Tom, and Kirtin Downey. 1992. "South Carolina May Have to Pay Compensation in Property Case." *Washington Post* (June 30):A10.

King, David C. 1994. "The Nature of Congressional Committee Jurisdictions." *American Political Science Review*. 88:48-62.

King, David C. 1997. *Turf Wars: How Congressional Committees Claim Jurisdiction*. Chicago: The University of Chicago Press.

King, Paula J. 1988. "Policy Entrepreneurs: Catalysts in the Policy Innovation Process." Ph.D. dissertation: University of Minnesota.

Kingdon, John W. 1995. *Agendas, Alternatives, and Public Policies*. 2nd ed. New York: Harper Collins College Publishers.

Kmiec, Douglas W. March 1997. "Inserting the Last Remaining Pieces into the Takings Puzzle." *William and Mary Law Review*. 38:995-1046.

Kmiec, Douglas W. 2001a. "Are Post-Enactment Purchasers of Regulated Land Without Remedy for Regulatory Takings?" *ABA Preview of US Supreme Court Cases*. 5(February):244.

Kmiec, Douglas W. 2001. "The Many Faces of Equal Treatment." *ABA Preview of US Supreme Court Cases*. 8(August):428.

Knickerbocker, Brad. 1993. "Property Rights Movement Gains Ground in Congress." *Christian Science Monitor*. (September) 21: 1.

Knox, Margaret L. 1993. "The World According to Cushman." *Wilderness*. 56:28.

Krehbiel, Keith. 1991. *Information and Legislative Organization*. Ann Arbor: University of Michigan Press.

Krehbiel, Keith, Kenneth A. Shepsle, and Barry R. Weingast. 1987. "Why Are Congressional Committees Powerful?" *American Political Science Review*. 81:929-45.

Kriz, Margaret. 1993. "Land Mine." *National Journal*. 25 (October 23): 2531-34.

Larson, Stephanie and David Grier. 1990. "Agenda Setting and AIDs". Paper prepared for presentation at the Annual Meeting of the American Political Science Association, San Francisco, California, August 29-September 2.

Latham, Earl. 1952. *The Group Basis of Politics*. Ithica, NY: Cornell University Press.

Lavelle, Marianne. 1995. "Activist Counties Battle the Federal Government Over Land Use Controls." *National Law Journal*. 7(June 5).

Levine, Michael C. 1999. "How Permanent Became Temporary in *Del Monte Dunes*." *Duke Law Journal*. 49(December):803.

Lieberman, Stuart J. 1997. "Court Weighs Final-Decision Rule in Takings Case." *The New Jersey Lawyer*. (August): 10.

Light, Paul C. 1982. *The President's Agenda*. Baltimore: John Hopkins University Press.

Limbaugh, Rush N. 1992. *The Way Things Ought to Be*. New York: Pocket Books.

Lipford, Jody and Donald J. Boudreaux. 1995. "The Political Economy of State Takings Legislation," in Bruce Yandle. ed. *Land Rights: The 1990's Property Rights Rebellion*. Lanham, MD.: Rowman and Littlefield Publishers, INC.

Lund, Hertha L. January 1995. "Property Rights Legislation in the States: A Review." *PERC Policy Series*. Issue Number PS-1. http://www.imt.net/~perc/ps1.htm

Lyons, Cody. May 5, 1999. Telephone Interview.

Mann, Eric. 1990. "Environmentalism in the Corporate Climate." *Tikkun*. 5(February).

Marzulla, Nancie G. 1995. "The Property Rights Movement: How It Began and Where It Is Headed." in Bruce Yandle. ed. *Land Rights: The 1990s' Property Rights Rebellion.* Lanham, MD.: Rowman and Littlefield.

Marzulla, Nancie G. 1999. Testimony before the U.S. House of Representatives, Committee on Resources, April 14, 1999. Taken from http://www.defenderspoprights.org/testimony.html.

Marzulla, Roger J. 1988. "The New Takings Executive Order and Environmental Regulation—Collision or Cooperation?" *Environmental Law Reporter.* (July):10254-60.

McCool, Dan. 1990. "Subgovernments as Determinants of Political Viability." *Political Science Quarterly.* 105: 269-293.

McCutcheon, Chuck et al. 1996. "Lott Tells Lobbyists Property Rights Bill is Dead for This Year." *CQ Monitor.* (September 9):5.

McFarland, Andrew S. 1991. "Interest Groups and Political Time: Cycles in America." *British Journal of Political Science.* 21:257-284.

Mintrom, Michael. 1997. "Policy Entrepreneurs and the Diffusion of Innovation." *American Journal of Political Science.* 41:738-770.

Mitchell, Robert Cameron. 1984. "Public Opinion and Environmental Politics in the 1970s and 1980s," in Norman J. Vig and Michael E. Kraft. eds. *Environmental Policy in the 1980s: Reagan's New Agenda.*Washington, DC: CQ Press.

Mitchell, Robert, Angela Mertig, and Riley Dunlap. 1985. "National Environmental Organizations." *Society and Natural Resources.* 4.

Moffett, Randolph R. 1996. "Regulatory Takings: Lobbying, Coalitions, and Influence." Ph.D. dissertation: West Virginia University.

Morin, Richard. 1995. "A Lighter Shade of Green." *Washington Post National Weekly Edition.* (June 5-11):37.

Moulton, Barbara. 1995. "Takings Legislation: Protection of Property Rights or Threat to the Public Interest?" *Environment*. 37(March):44-45.

Orren, Karen. 1991. *Belated Feudalism*. Cambridge: Cambridge University Press.

O'Keefe, Michael, and Kevin Daley. 1993. "Checking the Right." *Buzzworm, The Environmental Journal*. 5(May/June).

Paehlke, Robert. 1989. *Environmentalism and the Future of Progressive Politics*. New Haven: Yale University Press.

Pennsylvania Coal v. Mahon, 260 US 393, 416. 1922.

Peters, B. Guy, and Brian W. Hogwood. 1985. "In Search of the Issue Attention Cycle." *Journal of Politics*. 47:239-53.

Pinchot, Gilford. 1947. *Breaking New Ground*. New York: Harcourt, Brace.

Plotkin, Sidney. 1987. *Keep Out: The Struggle for Land Use Control*. Berkeley, CA.: University of California Press.

Polsby, Nelson W. 1984. *Policy Innovation in America: The Politics of Policy Innovation*. New Haven: Yale University Press.

Rabe, Barry G. 1997. "Power to the States: The Promise and Pitfalls of Decentralization," in Norman J. Vig and Michael E. Kraft. eds. *Environmental Policy in the 1990s*. Washington D.C.: CQ Press

Radford, RS. 1999. "The Constitutional Status of TDRs in the Aftermath of *Suitum*." *Stetson Law Review*. 28(Winter)685.

Ray, Dixy Lee and Lou Guzzo. 1993. *Environmental Overkill: Whatever Happened to Common Sense?* Washington D.C.: Regnery Gateway.

Riker, William. 1986. *The Art of Political Manipulation*. New Haven: Yale University Press.

Rosenbaum, Walter A. 1995. *Environmental Politics and Policy.* Washington DC: CQ Press.

Rosenbaum, Walter A. 1998. *Environmental Politics and Policy.* 4th ed. Washington DC: CQ Press.

Sabatier, Paul A. and Hank C. Jenkins-Smith. 1993. *Policy Change and Learning: An Advocacy Coalition Approach.* Boulder: Westview Press.

Salisbury, David F. 1981. "Energy: The Varmit That May Spoil America's West." *The Christian Science Monitor.* (September 3):B26.

Savage, David G. 2002. "No Time Out for Taking." *ABA Journal.* 88(January):27.

Sax, Joseph L. 1971. "Takings, Private Property and Public Rights." *The Yale Law Journal.* 81:149.

Sax, Joseph L. 1996. "Takings Legislation: Where it Stands and What Is Next." *Ecology Law Quarterly.* 23:509-520.

Schattschneider, E. E. 1960. *The Semisoveriegn People: A Realist's View of Democracy in America.* New York: Holt, Rinehart, and Winston.

Schlesinger, Arthur M. Jr. 1986. *The Cycles of American History.* Boston: Houghton Mifflin.

Shabecoff, Philip. 1993. *A Fierce Green Fire.* New York: Hill and Wang.

Shepsle, Kenneth A. 1978. *The Giant Jigsaw Puzzle.* Chicago: University of Chicago Press.

Shepsle, Kenneth A. 1979. "Institutional Arrangements and Equilibrium in Multidimensional Voting Models." *American Journal of Political Science.* 23:27-60.

Short, Brant C. 1989. *Ronald Reagan and the Public Lands: America's Conservation Debate.* College Station: Texas A&M University Press.

Smith, James A. 1991. *The Idea Brokers.* New York: Free Times Press.

Smith, Steven S., and Christopher Deering. 1990. *Committees in Congress.* Washington, DC: Congressional Quarterly.

Smith, Zachary A. 1995. *The Environmental Policy Paradox.* 2nd ed. Englewood Cliffs, N.J.: Prentice Hall, Inc.

Snider, MacWilliams Cosgrove. 1993. *The Wise Use Movement: Strategic Analysis and the Fifty State Review.* Washington, D.C.: Environmental Working Group. March:1,27.

Stedfast, Susan M. 1999. "Takings Law Symposium: Regulatory Takings: A Historical Overview and Legal Analysis for Natural Resources Management." *Environmental Law.* 29(Winter):881.

Steinhart, Carol, and John Steinhart. 1972. *Blowout: A Case Study of the Santa Barbara Oil Spill.* Belmont, CA: Wadsworth.

Switzer, Jacqueline Vaughn. 1997. *Green Backlash.* Lynne Reinner Publishers, Boulder.
Switzer, Jacqueline Vaughn. 1994. *Environmental Politics: Domestic and Global Dimensions.* New York: St. Martin's Press.

Symons, Lee P. 1988. "Property Rights and Local Land Use Regulation: The Implications of *First English* and *Nollan*." *Publius* 18: 81-95.

Talbert, Jeffery C., Bryan D. Jones, and Frank R. Baumgartner. 1995. "Nonlegislative Hearings and Policy Change in Congress." *American Journal of Political Science* 39:383-406.

Thurber, James. 1991. "Dynamics of Subsystems in American Politics." In Allan Cigler and Burdett Loomis, eds. *Interest Group Politics.* 3rd edition. Washington, DC: Congressional Quarterly Press.

Teifer, Charles. 1994. *The Semi-Sovereign Presidency.* Boulder: Westview.

Treanor, William Michael. March 1997. "The Armstrong Principle, the Narratives of Takings, and Compensation Statutes." *William and Mary Law Review.* 38:1151-1176.

Truman, David. 1951. *The Governmental Process.* New York: Alfred A. Knopf.

U.S. Environmental Protection Agency, 1990. *Environmental Investments: The Costs of a Clean Environment.* EPA-230-11-90-083, November. Washington D.C.: EPA.

Vig, Norman J. 1997. "Presidential Leadership and the Environment: From Reagan to Clinton," in Norman J. Vig and Michael E. Kraft. eds. *Environmental Policy in the 1990s.* 3rd ed. Washington D.C.: Congressional Quarterly Press.

Walker, Jack L. 1969. "The Diffusion of Innovations Among the American States." *American Political Science Review.* 63:880-899.

Walker, Jack L. 1991. *Mobilizing Interest Groups in America: Patrons, Professions, and Social Movements.* Ann Arbor, MI: The University of Michigan Press.

Wasylik, Alex Michael. June 19, 1999. Author's Interview, Washington, D.C.

Welch, Lee Ann. 1995. "Property Rights Conflicts Under the Endangered Species Act: Protection of the Red-Cockaded Woodpecker," in Bruce Yandle. ed. *Land Rights.* Lanham M.D.: Rowman & Littlefield Publishers.

Wenner, Lettie McSpadden and Lee E. Dutter. 1988. "Contextual Influences on Court Outcomes." *Western Political Quarterly.* 41:415-434.

Wilson, Woodrow. 1885, 1973. *Congressional Government: A Study in American Politics.* Gloucester, MA: Peter Smith.

Wise, Charles, R. 1992. "The Changing Doctrine of Regulatory Taking and the Executive Branch." *Administrative Law Review.* 44(Spring):404.

Worsham, Jeffrey. 1997. *Other People's Money: Policy Change, Congress, and Bank Regulation.* Boulder: Westview Press.

Worsham, Jeff. 1998. "Wavering Equilibriums: Subsystem Dynamics and Agenda Control." *American Politics Quarterly.* October: 485-512.

INDEX

agenda control, 6, 18, 20, 86, 117
agenda setting, 2, 5, 6, 8-17, 22, 25, 74-77, 81, 87-89, 117, 118, 131
agenda types, 6
Agins test, 58-61, 67, 124
Agins v. City of Tiburon, 53, 57-58

Baumgartner and Jones, 8, 11, 15-19, 89-93, 117, 128, 145

City of Monterey v. Del Monte Dunes, 64-68
Clean Water Act, 31-32
Cobb, Ross, and Ross, 8, 10
countermobilization, *See* Schattschneider

decision agenda, 8, 11, 20, 27, 87, 88, 111
Dolan v. City of Tigard, 61-62
Downs, 15

"economically viable" criteria and takings, 58-60, 72, 118, 124

eminent domain, 1, 46, 47, 95, 101, 102, 103, 104, 105, 106, 114, 95, 104, 145, 146
eminent domain assessment legislation (EDA), 101-104
eminent domain compensation legislation (EDC), 102-103
endangered species, 32-33

environmental movement, 2, 22-25, 27-29, 34-37

Fifth Amendment, 1, 45, 57, 62, 63, 66
First English Evangelical Lutheran Church of Glendale v County of Los Angeles, 55-56
Fourteenth Amendment, 1, 51, 65

government agenda, 7, 26, 87

hearing venue, 86-100
Herfindahl index, 94-95

jury trial in takings cases, *See* Fourteenth Amendment

Keystone Bituminous Coal Association v DeBenedictus, 53-54
Kingdon, 12-13

legislative referrals, 76-86
Lucas v South Carolina Coastal Council, 59-60

Nollan v California Coastal Commission, 56-57

Palazzolo v Rhode Island, 68-70
Pennsylvania Central Transportation Company v New York, 52-53

Pennsylvania Coal v Mahon,
50-52
political cycles, *See*
Baumgartner and Jones

property rights, 2, 5, 20-22, 26-32, 37-39, 44-50, 54-58, 64, 71-79, 86, 89, 95-97, 100-132
property rights legislation, types of, 100-104
property rights movement, *See* property rights
punctuated equilibrium, *see* Baumgartner and Jones

regulatory takings, 3-4, 17, 33, 62, 66, 72, 117, 120

Sage Brush Rebellion, 39-41
Schattschneider, 10, 16-18, 21, state level takings legislation, 121-131

Suitum v Tahoe Regional Planning Agency, 62-64
systemic agenda, 6-7, 10-11, 23-25

Tahoe-Sierra Preservation Council v Tahoe Regional Planning Agency, 70-71
taking assessment legislation (TA), 104
Takings Clause, 1, 154
takings compensation legislation (TC), 104-105
"too far" edict,
transferable development rights (TDR), 62-64

venue, *See* Baumgartner and Jones

wetlands, 28-33
Wise Use Movement, 41-44